W9-CLB-686

DEBATED
ANIMAL
RIGHTS

AMERICAN ISSUES

DEBATED

ANIMAL RIGHTS

Herbert M. Levine

RSVP
RAINTREE
STECK-VAUGHN
PUBLISHERS
The Steck-Vaughn Company

Austin, Texas

For Larry and Gayle Dinerstein

Published by Raintree Steck-Vaughn Publishers, an imprint of Steck-Vaughn Company
Publishing Director: Walter Kossmann
Graphic Design & Project Management: Gino Coverty
Editors: Kathy DeVico, Shirley Shalit
Photo Editor: Margie Foster
Electronic Production: Gino Coverty

Library of Congress Cataloging-in-Publication Data
Levine, Herbert M.
Animal rights / Herbert M. Levine.
p. cm.—(American issues debated)
Includes bibliographical references and index.
Summary: Debates topics such as banning the use of animals in scientific testing, the wearing of fur, and even whether or not the modern animal rights movement is good for America.
ISBN 0-8172-4350-X
1. Animal rights--United States-- Juvenile literature.
2. Animal welfare--Moral and ethical aspects--United States--Juvenile literature.
[1. Animal Rights.   2. Animals--Treatment.]
I. Title.   II. Series.
HV4764.L48   1998
179'.3--dc21   97-1223
                              CIP
                              AC

Printed and bound in the United States
1 2 3 4 5 6 7 8 9 0 LB 01 00 99 98 97

Photograph Acknowledgments
Cover: © David Sailors/The Stock Market; p. 7 © P. F. Bentley/Black Star; p. 13 Corbis-Bettmann; p. 17 Reuters/Brian Snyder/Archive Photos; p. 21 © John Troja/Black Star; p. 30 Park Street; p. 35 © MarkClarke/Science Photo Library/Photo Researchers; p. 39 © Ron Shohs/Black Star; p. 48 © Michael Fredericks/Animals Animals; p. 51 © Joe Munroe/Photo Researchers; p. 54 © Phillip Hayson/Photo Researchers; p. 58 © Mike Andrew/Animals Animals; p. 61 © Jim W. Grace/Photo Researchers; p. 64 © W. J. Schoonmaker/Photo Researchers; p. 67 © C. C. Lockwood/Animals Animals; p. 71 © Gary W. Griffen/Animals Animals; p. 72 © Eric & David Hosking/Photo Researchers; p. 76 © Allsport; p. 78 © Porterfield/Chickering/Photo Researchers; p. 82 UPI/Corbis-Bettmann; p. 86 © Corbis; p. 87 © Jim Barr/Gamma Liaison; p. 90 © Michael Nichols/Magnum Photos; p. 93 © Barbara Rios/Photo Researchers; p. 95 © Reuters/Peter Morgan/Archive Photos; p. 105 © Gamma-Liaison; p. 109 © Reuters/Peter Morgan/Archive Photos; p. 114 © C. C. Lockwood/Animals Animals.

CONTENTS

1. The World of Animal Rights.............6
Animal Rights and Animal Welfare
Animal Rights in Historical Perspective

2. Animals in Science 20
Debate: Should Animals Be Banned from Use in Science?

3. Animal Agriculture 44
Debate: Should Animal Agriculture Be Ended?

4. Hunting Animals 60
Debate: Should Hunting Be Illegal?

5. Animals in Entertainment.............75
Debate: Should Animals Be Released from Zoos and Aquariums and Returned to the Wild?

6. Furry Animals 91
Debate: Should We Be Ashamed to Wear Fur?

7. Conclusion: The Consequences of Animal Rights.....101
Debate: Is the Modern Animal Rights Movement Good for America?

Abbreviations 117

Glossary 118

Bibliography 120

Further Reading................124

Index 125

Chapter 1
THE WORLD OF ANIMAL RIGHTS

Animal Rights and Animal Welfare
Animal Rights in Historical Perspective

On the day after Thanksgiving—the busiest shopping day of the year—hundreds of demonstrators in several American cities gather outside of fur shops and department stores to denounce the sale of furs. They carry signs and distribute leaflets with messages, such as "You Should Be Ashamed to Wear Fur" and "Dead Animals Aren't Pretty." They display gruesome pictures of bleeding, furry animals twisting in pain as their legs are caught in steel traps. They plead with would-be shoppers to bypass the stores that sell furs.

Some of these protesters get involved in political activism because of the way animals are caught or bred for the benefit of the fur industry. They object to the killing of animals for the specific purpose of making expensive coats for wealthy people. But other protesters have a much broader plan than eliminating the commercial use of furs: They want to end human use of animals for all purposes.

Arguing that animals should have the same rights, or equivalent consideration, as humans, they support a philosophy of animal rights. Although supporters of animal rights differ among themselves about the reasons why ethical, or moral, behavior requires humans to grant rights to animals, most of them agree that just as humans have no right to own or use a fellow human being (such as in slavery), so, too, humans have no right to own or use an animal.

Since human beings use animals in many ways, animal rights supporters favor a massive change in our society. In a world guided by the philosophy of animal rights, humans could not use animals for scientific purposes, such as in laboratory experimentation to advance knowledge about diseases, or in the manufacture of vaccines, or in the safety testing of products for human use.

Animal rights supporters are not only against the use of animals for scientific purposes, but they oppose the entire animal agriculture industry, as well. That is to say, humans should not use animals for food. Specifically, the banning of animal agriculture would mean that humans would eat no animal flesh, such as meat, poultry, or fish, nor would humans eat animal products, such as milk and eggs. Animal rights control in society would also mean no use of animals for other purposes, such as the manufacture of leather shoes, fur coats, and wool sweaters.

According to the animal rights view, humans have no right to hunt or trap animals for food, clothing, or sport. Animal rightists also oppose zoos and aquariums because they feel that no matter

Supporters of animal rights protest the use of animals for scientific experiments conducted in the labs at the University of California at Berkeley.

how noble the intentions of the animal caretakers, humans have no right to hold animals in captivity. In such a view, humans have no right to even capture endangered types of animals for the purpose of restoring them to the wild.

The animal rights position is hostile to circuses, rodeos, horse and dog racing, and horse-drawn carriage rides. It opposes the breeding of particular kinds of animals, such as Irish setters. And it condemns the sale of animals in pet stores.

Animal rightists object to the very term pet, because it assumes human control over animals. Many animal rightists believe that ethical behavior permits a human to adopt an animal from the animal pound and take the animal into his or her home. In this way, the animal is rescued from death. The animal is then a companion animal, but not a pet. Companion implies equality of species, and pet implies human dominance of animals. (An animal species is a biological class of animals with common features.) Animal rightists oppose the use of animals as guide dogs to assist blind humans and specially trained anti-bomb or antidrug dogs to help the police in their work, too.

The animal rights position on specific issues, ranging from science to entertainment, reflects a philosophy guided by a hostility to speciesism, which is a philosophy asserting the exclusive interests of the human species over the nonhuman species. The term speciesism was coined in 1971 by Richard Ryder, a campaigner for animal rights who became chairman of the Royal Society for the Prevention of Cruelty to Animals (RSPCA) in Great Britain. Many supporters of animal rights contend that speciesism is as wicked as racism—a philosophy that holds that one race is superior to another—or sexism—a philosophy that asserts that one gender is superior to another.

Both supporters and opponents of animal rights agree that if the animal rights program is adopted, it will have serious consequences in the way we live. The nature of these consequences in such matters as ethical behavior, health, economic development, physical safety, medical research, conservation, and the quality of life for humans and animals is a matter of continuing dispute and importance.

Because the stakes are so high for both humans and animals, the subject of animal rights deserves study. This book is an introduction to the study of animal rights. It begins by examining the ideas underlying animal rights and the historical development of the animal rights movement.

Rather than presenting a single point of view about animal rights, the book offers opposing sides on a few of the major issues about the subject. Those issues deal with science, agriculture, hunting, entertainment, and furs. The book concludes with an estimate of the consequences of the animal rights movement to American society.

Animal Rights and Animal Welfare

As indicated earlier, animal rights is a philosophy that claims animals should have rights or interests equal to those of humans. People who advocate this view understand that animals could not possibly possess all the rights that humans possess because animals are different from humans. No one argues, for example, that an animal should have the right to vote. But, according to the animal rights view, people should at the minimum give equal consideration to the interest of animals as they do to that of humans.

To understand the meaning of animal rights and terms associated with this philosophy, we have to explain some definitions and ideas. Although by definition a human being is technically one kind of animal, we will distinguish between human and nonhuman animals. As used in this book, the term animal includes nonhuman creatures, such as horses, cows, and mice as well as fish, frogs, and chickens. Some animals have many biological features similar to those of humans. Chimpanzees are more like humans than are any other animals. Other animals, such as insects, have so few similarities to humans that some animal rightists do not include them as central to the subject of animal rights.

So much for the term animal. But what about the term rights? A right may be defined as a just claim. That is to say, if a person has a right to vote, he or she may not legally be prevented from casting a ballot. Political systems that respect rights support not only the right to vote but also other rights, such as the right to voice opinions, practice a religious faith, and be assured a fair trial in a criminal case.

One of the most important rights in a democratic political system is the right to personal liberty. In this system, the state may not legally take away a person's liberty without due process—that is, without abiding by constitutional guarantees against the arbitrary taking of life, liberty, or property. In a system based on rights, a person may not legally be forced to be used in an experiment in medical research without his or her consent, for example.

But no country today has a system that gives animals the same legal right to life as it gives to humans. So a medical researcher can use an animal in an experiment as the researcher wants (although most countries have laws and regulations governing the treatment and use of animals for scientific purposes). And a farmer may slaughter cattle to feed his or her family without fear of being arrested.

In an animal rights world, such practices would be abolished or at least be greatly limited. Animal rights supporters believe that it is the right of animals to be left alone by humans. The personal freedom of animals to be safe from confinement or exploitation would be assured if the animal rights view of the world prevailed. By exploitation is meant any cruel or unjust use of animals for the personal advantage of humans.

Such a view of animal rights is in contrast to animal welfare—the view that humans possess a right to own or use animals but must do so in a humane way. People who are in favor of animal welfare declare that humans are the stewards of the animal kingdom. In other words, humans possess the right to own or control animals since humans are superior to animals. Humans, therefore, may kill animals for food, clothing, or scientific research and may use them for entertainment.

But animal welfare supporters argue that although humans have a right to use animals, they have no right to abuse them. By abuse, they mean to cause unnecessary harm. An example of abuse would be to torture an animal solely for the sake of seeing it die. Animal welfarists would permit the slaughtering of animals for food, for example, but only if done in a manner that causes the least amount of suffering to the animals.

In summary, animal rightists believe that humans have no right to cause animals to suffer. Animal welfarists believe that humans have authority over animals and, consequently, may be permitted to cause animals minimal suffering. Although animal rightists and animal welfarists sometimes work together to protest what they consider to be the inhumane exploitation of animals, the two philosophies are by nature in conflict. Animal welfarists seek to reform current practices of animal use; animal rightists want to abolish all human use of animals.

The animal rights view of the world is controversial and has produced much opposition. The harshest critics of animal rights say that it is impossible to include animals in any serious discussion of rights. These critics differ about why animals are not entitled to have rights. One group of critics argues along religious lines. They say that God created humans in God's image; God did not create animals that way. They point to passages in the Old Testament, the New Testament, and the Koran to justify their views.

A second group makes its case in terms of natural law—that is, laws that are fundamental to human nature. This group asserts that humans have inalienable rights, like the rights of life, liberty, and the pursuit of happiness mentioned in the Declaration of Independence. These rights exist for the benefit of humans, and not for animals.

A third group contends that the idea of rights is a human creation founded by people who have the ability to think reasonably and act morally. In this way of looking at rights, this group maintains that only humans have the capacity to make moral judgments. Supporters of this view say that anyone who claims rights takes on responsibilities, as well. If a person expects to have his or her freedom of speech protected, then he or she is under the moral obligation, or duty, to respect the freedom of speech of others. Animals cannot have rights because they cannot accept responsibilities, according to this third group of critics.

Critics of animal rights do not object when they are accused of being speciesists. "Of course, we are speciesists," they argue. And then they add, "But so, too, are animals who mate with creatures of their own kind and secure their own territory."

Animal Rights in Historical Perspective

For the most part, notions of special consideration for animals are a development of the past two centuries in the countries of the western world. The western philosophical tradition holds that people may regard animals as possessing an inferior moral position to humans. From ancient times to the present, however, some individuals and groups expressed concern for the well-being of animals. For example, St. Francis of Assisi, the 13th-century Italian monk, revered nature and the world of animals.

In the past few centuries, one of the earliest philosophers to deal with the issue of the human treatment of animals was Jeremy Bentham, an English philosopher. In his *Introduction to the Principles of Morals and Legislation* (published in 1789), he wrote: "The question is not, can they [animals] reason? Nor, can they talk? But can they suffer?" The Bentham view was in sharp conflict with the popular view of philosophical thinking of the times. The French philosopher René Descartes voiced the accepted view by claiming that animals were incapable of feeling pain.

The work of Charles Darwin, the 19th-century English naturalist who wrote about evolution (the belief that existing organisms descended from a common ancestor), influenced the way humans think about animals. Darwin said that the only difference between humans and other animals was a difference of degree, not kind.

Concern with the human treatment of animals was expressed most notably in Great Britain and the United States in the 19th and 20th centuries. The early interest centered on doing away with cruelty to animals and ending or regulating the use of animals in scientific research. For the most part, the movement was in the tradition of animal welfare rather than animal rights.

In 1822, Great Britain passed the first law to protect animals. In 1824, William Wilberforce and Sir Thomas Fowell Buxton, two leaders of the British anti-slave-trade movement, helped found the Society for the Prevention of Cruelty to Animals, which later received the approval of Queen Victoria and became the Royal Society for the Prevention of Cruelty to Animals (RSPCA). The purpose of the organization was to help protect animals from unnecessarily harsh treatment. In 1876, Great Britain passed the Cruelty to Animals Act, requiring animal researchers to obtain government licenses for experiments that would mean causing pain to vertebrates (animals having a backbone or spinal column).

In the United States, the movement for animal protection began in 1866 when Henry Bergh founded the American Society for the Prevention of Cruelty to Animals (ASPCA). In 1870, New York adopted laws making cruelty to animals a misdemeanor, a crime that is considered more of a misdeed than a serious offense. By 1907, every state in the United States had some form of legislation protecting animals from cruel treatment. In 1883, the American Anti-Vivisection Society, which sought the regulation of vivisection—the dissecting or experimenting with live animals for medical research—was founded in Philadelphia.

Henry Bergh founded the ASPCA in 1866. The organization had the authority to stop local practices that were cruel to animals.

The international animal rights movement was founded by Henry Salt with the publication in 1892 of his *Animals' Rights Considered in Relation to Human Progress.* By the end of the 19th century, most western countries passed laws against the cruel treatment of animals.

In the first few decades of the 20th century, the movement concerned with animal protection lost support. Scientists organized to fight efforts to curb the use of animals in their work. Because scientists conducted animal research that led to the production of vaccines for the treatment of diseases such as rabies, efforts to limit scientists did not gain much popular approval.

After World War II, however, the animal protection movement gained new strength in the United States and in other countries. In the 1950s, several animal protection groups were founded in the United States, including the Animal Welfare Institute in 1951, the Humane Society of the United States (HSUS) in 1954, and Friends of Animals in 1957.

Because of popular feeling in favor of reform in the treatment of animals, legislation was enacted. The federal Humane Slaughter Act of 1958 required meat-packers to use ways of eliminating pain in the slaughter of animals. And in 1966, Congress passed the Laboratory Animal Welfare Act, requiring the licensing of dealers and registration of laboratories. It also set some standards for the care of animals. This was the first law to deal with the care and treatment of animals in scientific laboratories. The law, which became known as the Animal Welfare Act (AWA), placed greater restrictions on researchers and animal dealers through amendments in 1970, 1976, and 1985.

The modern animal protection movement gained enormously from two scholarly works supporting the interests of animals. The first was the publication in 1985 of *Animal Liberation* by Peter Singer, an Australian philosopher. Singer's book and his other writings argue from a point of view known as utilitarianism—a philosophy that holds that a moral act should be judged on the basis of its consequences. In other words, an act should be evaluated on the basis of whether it serves the greatest good for the greatest number.

In Singer's view, since animals experience suffering similar to that of humans, we ought to be careful about using animals to serve the exclusive interests of humans. Singer argues that humans should take into consideration the interests of animals in human associations with animals. Singer never actually claims that animals possess rights, however. He argues only that animal interests should be taken into consideration in any human use of animals. Singer was particularly against speciesism.

In contrast to the utilitarian approach of Peter Singer is the rights approach, often associated with philosopher Tom Regan. In *The Case for Animal Rights* (1984), Regan argues that animals should have rights not because of their capacity to suffer, but rather because they are the "subject of a life." A subject of a life possesses features such as memory, beliefs, preferences, emotional states, an identity, and a definable welfare. One important right for a subject of a life is the right to life. Any animal that is capable of having beliefs and desires should not be used by humans for their own selfish purposes. So humans cannot use animals even for the most worthy ends, according to Regan's view.

Singer and Regan became the principal philosophers of the animal rights movement in the 1970s. That movement has grown stronger since that time. In 1976, Henry Spira, a former high school teacher, became an expressive and forceful participant in the movement. He protested animal experiments sponsored by the American Museum of Natural History in New York City with money from the National Institutes of Health (NIH), a federal government institution sponsoring health research projects.

Spira, who was an activist in the labor union and civil rights movement, revealed that the museum-sponsored experimenters planned to deafen, blind, and destroy the sense of smell of cats by removing parts of their brains for the stated purpose of observing changes in the mating habits of cats. The goal was to apply the information learned from these experiments to human experience.

Spira led demonstrations against the research every weekend for 18 months, complaining that the experiments were cruel and would not relieve any human pain. The publicity caused by these demonstrations hurt the reputation of the museum. NIH stopped paying for the experiments after 121 members of Congress raised questions about their usefulness. The laboratory conducting the experiments then closed.

In 1978, Spira turned his attention to Revlon, a major cosmetics company. He tried to get Revlon to stop testing its products and cosmetic ingredients on rabbits. (See Chapter 2.) Revlon would not answer his letters, so he took out advertisements in a newspaper in 1980 asking: "How many rabbits does Revlon blind for beauty's sake?"

Since Revlon sells beauty products and depends for its success on its image of creating beauty, it saw how damaging the publicity was. The company changed its policy. It also gave money to Rockefeller University for the purpose of encouraging research on finding alternatives to animal testing.

After his success in dealing with Revlon, Spira urged other cosmetics companies to follow Revlon's example. Avon, in turn, began giving money to the Center for Alternatives to Animal Testing (CAAT) at Johns Hopkins University. A group of cosmetic companies, the Cosmetic, Toiletry, and Fragrance Association, gave $1 million to establish CAAT. Most of the major cosmetics companies, including Revlon, Avon, and Estée Lauder, have stopped animal testing.

The animal protection movement built on these successes and really gathered strength in the 1980s. In 1980, Ingrid Newkirk, a former Humane Society official, and Alex Pacheco, an activist with connections to the British animal rights movement, founded People for the Ethical Treatment of Animals (PETA). Their cause catapulted them and PETA to national notice as a result of a sensational story involving a science laboratory.

In 1981, Pacheco worked at the Institute for Behavioral Research in Silver Spring, Maryland, a suburb of Washington, D.C. He gathered information about experiments on 17 monkeys at the lab.

Claiming that the lab was mistreating the monkeys, he notified the police, who conducted a raid of the premises. This was the first occasion in the history of the United States in which police raided a scientific research laboratory because of charges of cruelty to animals.

The "Silver Spring Monkeys," as the animals seized in this raid were called, became the spark that set the protest movement afire. Dr. Edward Taub, who headed the research experiments, denied the charges that his lab was violating laws on animal treatment. Taub was convicted of cruelty to animals, but a Maryland court overturned the conviction. Although it took many years of legal contests, Taub succeeded in getting all charges dropped. But the publicity of the Silver Spring monkeys pushed PETA into the forefront of the animal rights movement.

In addition to PETA, many animal protection groups were formed in the 1980s. In 1981, George Cave and Dana Stuchell founded Trans-Species Unlimited. The name of the organization was changed to Animal Rights Mobilization in 1990. Other important animal protection groups founded in

Three PETA members dressed as rabbits unfurl a banner that reads "Gilette Tortures Animals" outside Gilette offices in Boston.

the 1980s were Californians for Responsible Research (which changed its name to become In Defense of Animals), and Animal Legal Defense Fund.

Because supporters and opponents of animal rights use the term animal rights in different ways—for example, as propaganda, as a proud emblem of a movement, as a symbol of a dishonorable cause—it is difficult to identify the groups that are animal rights organizations. It is easier and fairer to refer to groups with a commitment to animal care—whether animal rights or animal welfare—as animal protection groups. Such a definition includes many organizations that have great differences with each other over the philosophy and methods of the animal protection movement, but that are all interested in the relation of humans to animals.

Today, there are thousands of animal protection groups in the United States. Possibly, several hundred of these are animal rights. One estimate says that the number of animal rights groups in the United States has increased tenfold since 1980.

Animal protection groups range from the American Humane Association, which is interested mostly in caring for stray or abandoned animals, particularly dogs and cats, to PETA, which has a broad program covering every human activity involving the use of animals. A number of animal protection organizations focus on one narrow area, such as fur, primates, animal agriculture, or use of laboratory animals.

Most animal protection organizations take part in legal activities only. They are active in such democratic processes as participating in public debates, supporting political candidates favoring their position, raising money to promote the care of animals or the cause of animal protection, and educating the public. Some of the groups are particularly good at gaining publicity for their movement. PETA, for example, enlists the support of Hollywood celebrities for its cause.

But in some cases, advocates for animals take part in illegal activities, such as breaking and entering scientific laboratories and destroying property and research. Animal Liberation Front (ALF) is the best known of the violent groups. It is a secret organization, lacking a central authority. Anyone wishing to engage in break-ins for the cause of animal liberation can claim some link with ALF.

ALF was founded in England by Ronnie Lee in 1976, as an outgrowth of another group, Band of Mercy. This group committed acts of sabotage, such as setting fires and harassing hunters. ALF spread to many countries, including the United States. Among its most noted acts was the destruction in 1987 of an animal medical center at the University of California at Davis, causing more than $5 million worth of damage.

As mentioned, most animal protection supporters condemn violent actions either because violence is truly hateful to them or because of their concern that violence will lead to less public support for the cause of animal protection. But some animal rights supporters say that although they do not support violence, they sympathize with those people who are willing to risk their freedom for the cause of animals.

One of the consequences of the animal rights movement has been to energize the groups that are the targets of the movement. As early as 1908, the American Medical Association (AMA) established the Committee for the Protection of Animal Research to fight the antivivisection movement. The National Association for Biomedical Research and the Foundation for Biomedical Research were founded in 1979 in answer to the rise in animal rights activism.

Private business companies and trade associations dealing with cosmetics, animal agriculture, zoos and aquariums, circuses, rodeos, hunting, and furs have devoted an increasing amount of their attention and resources to defending their practices against the charges of animal protection organizations. At times, the opposing forces have tried to achieve their goals through government action—at the local, state, and national levels—and at the international level, too.

The conflict over the relationship between humans and animals is a continuing one and involves many areas of our lives. We will consider the more controversial issues in the following chapters.

Chapter 2
ANIMALS IN SCIENCE

Debate: Should Animals Be Banned from Use in Science?

• You visit Dr. Barbara Jones's office for a medical examination. Your doctor uses X rays, a blood test, and other means to judge your health.

• You go to the pharmacy and buy the prescription that your doctor has told you to take for your medical problem.

• While waiting for your prescription, you buy some soap and shampoo.

• You return home and turn on your television set. You watch the launching of a manned rocket to outer space.

Not mentioned in any of these scenes are animals. But they are there in abundance, and they tell much about the use of animals in science.

Your doctor may have had her first encounter with the scientific use of animals when she was a student in her high school biology class, where she dissected a frog to meet a laboratory-course requirement. In her later studies in college and medical school, she dissected not only a frog, but also other animals, such as mice and rats.

The prescription that your doctor wrote for you might have been for insulin, a medicine that is itself an animal product used to treat diabetes. It is a preparation derived from the pancreas of a pig or an ox. Researchers developed insulin in the 1950s. Pharmaceutical companies put the drug on the market in the 1960s after many tests—first on animals and then, when insulin was thought to be safe for animals, on human beings.

The shampoo and soap products you purchased are safe. Since these items could possibly harm your skin or damage your eyes, the manufacturers tested these products on animals before releasing them for public sale. The chances are that you never even considered safety as a reason for buying the two items. You just assumed the products were safe.

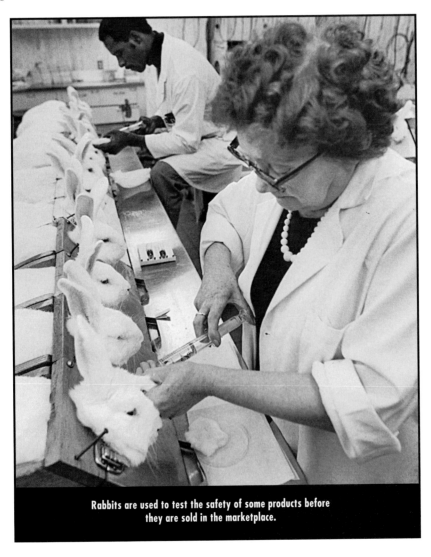

Rabbits are used to test the safety of some products before they are sold in the marketplace.

Finally, as you watch the rocket carrying the astronauts on a scientific mission, you sense the astronauts' joy of achievement and adventure. The screen fills up with pictures of the earliest space trips, but these trips were made not by astronauts, but by dogs and monkeys. You learn that after careful checking of the effect of space travel on the vital organs of animals, scientists planned the best methods to assure the safety of humans for similar and even more daring trips.

Scientists use millions of animals in their research every year. The exact number of animals used for scientific purposes in the United States is not certain. Estimates vary from 14 million to 100 million. Among these animals are rats, mice, dogs, cats, chickens, rabbits, and even primates, such as monkeys and chimpanzees. Animals are used in science mostly in three ways: in research and medication, education, and product safety testing.

Research and medication. Although the use of animals in science is at least 2,000 years old, it is mostly a feature of the 19th and 20th centuries. Vivisection is now a common practice in science although it is a practice that has brought strong objections.

Medical researchers rely on laboratory animals to discover the effects of new medications and procedures on the health and behavior of animals before the researchers experiment on human beings. When the tests fail to produce results that scientists seek, they end—or change—their tests. When the tests produce promising results, the scientists ask for approval from their superiors to conduct similar tests on human beings. Sometimes, a test on a human being has the same result as a similar test on an animal. Often, however, the result is different.

Scientists have used and continue to use animals in all kinds of medical research, such as in the search for cures for rabies, cancer, polio, heart disease, stroke, diabetes, Parkinson's Disease, Acquired Immunodeficiency Syndrome (AIDS), and every other major illness or health problem. Researchers also use animals in research with human behavior, such as drug addiction, alcoholism, and criminal violence.

Pharmaceutical companies use animals to manufacture medicines. As mentioned above, insulin comes from pigs and oxen. Animal products make up many treatments for diseases other than diabetes and help make up the vaccines for such illnesses as polio, rubella, diphtheria, whooping cough, smallpox, tetanus, and yellow fever. Also, some doctors are working on experiments in xenography—the transplantation of healthy body parts of animals to humans with comparable, but diseased, body parts, such as the heart and the liver.

Education. The use of animals in education begins much earlier than medical school. Teachers in many high school biology classes and in college anatomy (the science of the body structure of plants and animals) classes often have students dissect frogs so that they will understand how the vital organs of this animal work. Medical school students dissect not only frogs, but also animals such as rabbits and cats. They also dissect cadavers (dead human beings).

Product safety testing. Since manufacturers of products are legally responsible for the products that they make, they need to be sure that the products are safe. Even nonmedical products, such as soap, shampoo, lipstick, facial lotion, shaving cream, and perfume, can cause skin irritation, allergies, or even blindness. Manufacturers often test these products—or sometimes their ingredients— on animals before they release their products for sale to the public.

That scientists have traditionally made great use of animals in their work is a fact. But major changes in technology, scientific knowledge, and ethical thinking raise questions about whether humans should use animals in science.

DEBATED:

SHOULD ANIMALS BE BANNED FROM USE IN SCIENCE?

Yes. The use of animals in science should be ended immediately. Animal research is unethical, barbaric, and unnecessary. It is obvious that animals would be better off if humans gave up animal research for scientific purposes. What medical researchers refuse to admit, however, is that humans would be better off, too.

Ethics. People who are earnest about leading an ethical life need to consider an animal as possessing the same right to life as a human being. Humans are more resourceful than animals because humans are capable of capturing, imprisoning, torturing, and killing animals. But this feature only makes humans powerful; it does not make them ethical. A big, heavy man can beat up a child; but if he does, he is only a bully and not a morally good person.

We can learn much about ethics when we study history. Until the U.S. Civil War, for example, white people in parts of the United States kept African Americans as slaves. Whites could break up families and deny legal rights to African Americans merely because of their skin color. At times, white people could legally injure and even kill African Americans. And white people could sell African Americans as if they were goods rather than human beings.

The Civil War decided the issue of slavery. The Thirteenth Amendment to the U.S. Constitution abolished slavery in 1865. However, discrimination against people because of their race continued. The nation adopted civil rights laws in the 19th and 20th centuries, and the principle of racial equality is accepted today by an overwhelming number of Americans. Americans who accept the principles of racial equality and live according to them are ethical. Those who do not are unethical.

We now have an ethical responsibility to broaden the application of the principles of civil rights. To some extent, we have already taken great strides in extending principles of civil rights to groups other than African Americans, such as women, Native Americans, the elderly, and physically disabled men and women. It is time for us to begin a new civil rights revolution—one based on a respect for all living creatures—whether human or animal. This revolution will rally around the idea that all living beings have fundamental rights that cannot be denied to them because of their species. If we accept this view, then speciesism will go the way of slavery in the coming decades as humankind moves to a more ethical standard of behavior.

Finally, we should keep in mind that animals are just like humans in many ways. In fact, a gorilla is 98.3 percent genetically identical to a human. A human is an animal, even according to the scientific classifications made by humans. Some animals have the ability to think and solve problems.

Speciesists say that the most important difference between an animal and a human is the human's ability to think and reason and to follow moral principles. However, these same thinkers neglect to consider human beings who lack these abilities, such as children and the mentally deficient. The law treats harshly human beings who abuse children and the mentally deficient. It does not allow humans to be subjected to painful, cruel, and deadly scientific laboratory experiments.

And yet, the law looks kindly on vivisectionists (those who perform vivisection) who torture and kill nonhuman animals, some of whom have a higher mental—and even moral—capacity than do some children and the mentally deficient. Vivisectionists pretend to a moral standard that they do not have when they apply their so-called right and good standards to animals that they are not willing to apply to their own kind.

If we want to follow ethical guides to our conduct, then we must respect the right of all living creatures, whether human or animal. Anything less than sticking to the principle of equality for all creatures is unacceptable for a moral being.

Barbarism. Vivisectionists go to great lengths to describe their treatment of animals in laboratories and in educational institutions as "humane," a term they would never apply to a similar treatment of humans. But even under the best conditions (best, that is, in the view of vivisectionists), the treatment of laboratory animals calls to mind the most ugly scenes from horror films of violence and evil. Here are some examples from legally approved experiments and other uses of animals for scientific purposes:

- In head-wound experiments, researchers shoot bullets into the heads of cats.

- In addiction studies, experimenters apply varying doses of addictive drugs, such as crack cocaine, into the bodies of monkeys until the mental ability of the animals is destroyed.

- Perfectly healthy baboons are kept in cages. Surgeons then kill the baboons and remove their livers, which are then transplanted into the bodies of human beings.

- For certain kinds of experiments, scientists drill holes into the heads of monkeys and implant electrodes into their brains.

These descriptions of medical research and treatment suggest images of horrible pain and cruelty. The examples of animal treatment in product safety testing offer even worse cases of the terror that humankind inflicts on animals. The Draize test and LD-50 are two cases in point.

The Draize test (named for Dr. John H. Draize of the Food and Drug Administration [FDA] who invented it) involves placing a substance into the eye of a live rabbit. First, the scientist removes the rabbit from a cage and puts the animal in a position that is firm so that the animal cannot move. Then the scientist pulls back the eyelids of the rabbit and inserts a measured dose of a suspected eye irritant. Scientists observe the rabbit from one to three days to examine for redness, blistering, bleeding, or blindness. That the substance can be poisonous and can cause pain and even blind an animal makes this test particularly cruel.

The "LD" of the LD-50 test stands for "lethal dose." In the classic LD-50 test, a dose of a test substance is gradually increased in the diets of 80 to 100 rats or mice until half of the animals die.

The animals subjected to scientific tests experience suffering, torture, and death. Many tests are unnecessary or are conducted for unimportant reasons. And many tests are for cosmetic items that are often only a slightly new variation of some existing vanity product, such as mascara or eye shadow.

Although some researchers and pharmaceutical and cosmetic manufacturers handle animals with careful attention to obeying government laws and regulations about the treatment of animals in their care, others do not. Often, the conditions of the laboratories are below the proper legal quality. To save money, private laboratories abuse animals and deny them even the minimum standards required by law. And some "caretakers" wickedly torture animals out of an evil sense of having fun, as undercover investigations conducted by animal rights groups show. When experiencing inadequate or cruel care, the animals suffer doubly—first, from living in unhealthy and cramped surroundings, and second, from subjection to scientific terror.

But even when vivisectionists obey the laws, they know that the laws are not effective enough to protect the animals. The AWA and its amendments (the principal federal laws governing animal care) furnish some help for the humane treatment of animals. These laws contain rules for deciding where animals can be obtained, for setting conditions by which they must be cared for during shipment and housing, and for establishing requirements governing the size of the cage in which they will be kept. But the AWA does not apply to all kinds of animals. For example, the law does not include protection for birds, horses, sheep, pigs, cattle, goats, rats, and mice. Nor does it cover fish, reptiles, or amphibians (frogs and toads). Omitting certain types of animals means that for 85 to 90 percent of animals used in laboratory research, the principal federal law does not apply. As a result, vivisectionists have what amounts to unspoken permission to kill and abuse a huge number of laboratory animals.

When vivisectionists take time out from pointing to laws governing their experimentation, they like to direct attention to government figures showing that fewer than 7 percent of animal experiments involve pain to an animal. Unfortunately for them (and for the truth), however, the way that institutions report experiments as painful varies from one research center to another. Some analysts report that certain institutions describe animal experiments as non-painful when they are in fact painful. We may conclude, therefore, that more research animals experience pain than federal government figures suggest.

It is not surprising that the way researchers treat animals is so careless and so lacking in compassion. The researchers are just continuing the kind of treatment to animals that their teachers allowed in the schools. Some of the worst examples of mistreatment of nonhuman creatures exist in the classrooms of secondary schools, colleges, and professional schools.

Two tests—involving observation and movement of the muscles of live frogs and the hearts of live turtles—are particularly brutal. The exercise requires each student to make the animal brain-dead by inserting a sharp object through the base of its head and into the braincase, and then moving the object in a manner to scramble the brain. Another exercise involves using a pair of scissors to cut off the head of a live frog. The purpose of these exercises is to allow students to see how the leg muscles of live frogs respond to electrical stimulation.

The record shows that animals in science endure great suffering. The experiments and testing are bad enough. Many of the animals caught or developed for science suffer from exhaustion and the drying out of body fluids. And some even die before they get to the labs or schools. Such treatment is surely barbaric.

Value of research. The scientific establishment argues that the use of animals in research is a necessary evil. But a close look at that research proves that most of it is unnecessary.

First, a good deal of animal research is of no practical use to humans. The biological structure of animals differs from that of humans. And medications and procedures that work successfully in animals may work poorly or not at all in humans. Let's look at just a few examples of these truths:

- Scientists use rabbits in the Draize test because the large size of the animals' eyes allows scientists to easily observe test results. But rabbits' eyes are different from human eyes in important ways, such as in the thickness of tissue structure. And rabbits tear less effectively than people.

- The artificial sweetener saccharin causes bladder cancer in rats but not in humans because the rat's bladder is significantly different from the human's bladder.

- When injected with human immunodeficiency virus (HIV), chimpanzees neither develop the symptoms of the typical HIV sufferer, nor do they get sick and die from HIV.

- Aspirin causes birth defects in rats and mice, is poisonous to cats, and fails to reduce fever in horses.

- Penicillin is highly toxic (poisonous) to guinea pigs and hamsters.

- Unleaded gasoline causes kidney tumors in male rats but not in female rats, mice, or humans.

- Morphine calms humans but excites cats.

- Benzine, a common industrial chemical, causes leukemia in humans, but not in mice.

- Arsenic produces cancer in humans but not in animals.

- The poison strychnine is fatal to humans but not to guinea pigs, chickens, or monkeys.

- Acetaminophen relieves pain and fever in humans, but it kills cats.

- Dogs, cats, rats, mice, and hamsters do not need Vitamin C, but a lack of it in humans, guinea pigs, and primates causes a serious disease called scurvy.

The case of the drug thalidomide is a notable example of how scientific knowledge about animals cannot be applied to humans. Doctors outside of the United States prescribed thalidomide in the 1960s for pregnant women suffering from nausea and vomiting, a condition common in the first three months of pregnancy. Thalidomide had been tested on mice in 14 separate animal experiments without producing birth defects in the offspring of those animals.

After thalidomide came on the market in Europe, health-care officials learned that the drug caused birth defects in humans. An estimated 10,000 infants were born with missing or shortened limbs and other defects. According to Dr. Gill Langley, "Thalidomide causes birth defects in humans at doses as low as 64 milligrams, but is harmless in some strains of rats at 4,000 times that amount." This case shows that research on animals cannot be applied to humans. Animal research, then, is of no scientific value to humans.

Common sense should tell us that when scientific researchers rely on animal research, they are bound to get poor results because they cannot understand the feelings of the animal. An animal cannot communicate with human beings in a way that humans will understand. For example, an animal cannot let a human know that it has double vision. Researchers may decide that an animal has a certain disease or condition when it displays the same behavior as a human with that disease. Then the scientist judges the animal's condition as he or she would judge a human's condition. That is a major scientific error in research.

Second, animal research is not needed because alternatives to animal research are available. These alternatives offer better scientific results than research based on experiments using animals. So long as practical alternatives can aid research, scientists ought to use them. The humane consequence of relying on alternatives is to spare the lives and prevent unnecessary torture and suffering of innocent animals. These alternatives include in vitro testing, clinical research, epidemiological studies, and computer modeling.

In vitro is a Latin term meaning "in glass" and usually refers to research that does not use live animals. In vitro research includes the use of bacteria, animal cells grown in a special mixture (cell culture), fertilized chicken eggs, or frog embryos. These can be studied in small glass dishes to evaluate the poisonous effects of chemicals in human beings. The Eytex system is an in vitro alternative to the Draize test and uses a combination of 53 proteins as much as exists in the makeup of the eye.

Partly as a result of improvements in cell-culture technology since the late 1970s, the National Cancer Institute has replaced its use of the mouse cancer model for screening for new drug treatments with cultures of human cancer cells. Three to four million mice a year are saved because of this change.

So perfected are the results of in vitro research that many of the biggest cosmetics companies are no longer testing ingredients or products on animals. These well-known companies include Avon, The Body Shop, Chanel, Christian Dior, Estée Lauder, M.A.C. Cosmetics, Neutrogena, and Revlon. Some of them proudly proclaim "cruelty free" on their product labels. If these companies have given up animal testing, then other manufacturers can do the same. Tests like the Draize and the LD-50 simply are no longer necessary to assure product safety.

Consumers concerned with animal rights make an effort to purchase products labeled "cruelty free" or "No Animal Testing."

Another alternative to animal research is clinical research, which involves analyzing the people who are ill with particular diseases. We have already shown that animals are different from humans in terms of their reaction to chemicals and medications. To find cures for human health problems, researchers should, therefore, study humans and not animals.

Epidemiological studies provide many insights into diseases. Such studies refer to investigations of naturally occurring disease patterns within populations. The result of one epidemiological study, for example, was the discovery of a connection between smoking and lung cancer.

Finally, computer modeling is a wonderful development of modern technology that can be as helpful in solving problems in medical research as it is in all kinds of other areas. In this book, computer modeling means the use of the computer to duplicate the features of humans or animals without having to experiment with humans or animals.

These alternative methods to animal research have produced great understanding of the factors and even the treatment of heart disease, Alzheimer's, cancer, and AIDS. Doctors who support animal rights are as determined as their adversaries to discover cures for diseases. And since the alternatives to animal research are practical, it is unethical to rely on more animal testing.

If alternatives to animal testing are available for medical research, they are also suitable for product safety. After all, animal testing does not prevent cosmetics- and household products-related injuries to about 70,000 Americans who are rushed to hospitals every year. Children are often the victims of consuming or touching such harmful products. To insure the safety of a product containing poisonous materials, a manufacturer could produce more child-resistant containers. Such a step would go a long way toward keeping children from coming into contact with dangerous materials. Animal experiments cannot prevent accidental poisoning, but child-resistant packages can.

Third, a reason for stopping animal research is that many uses of animal research just duplicate results that have already been found in earlier experiments. Scientists often conduct new tests because such tests mean more money in their pockets from grant-making agencies. These agencies, which are mostly in government, provide financial support for scientific research.

Even when the scientists are not greedy, however, many of them continue to experiment with animals because they have been trained to do this kind of work. It would cost them time, trouble, and money to return to medical school to learn new ways of researching.

Fourth, animal experiments encourage people to emphasize treatment rather than prevention. Such an emphasis truly harms public health. For example, many problems of poor health are caused by bad diets. If Americans ate healthier foods than the high-fat items that they now eat (like cheeseburgers, french fries, and malted milk), then they would be less likely to get disabling and deadly ailments, such as heart disease or cancer. Of the ten leading causes of death in the United States today, smoking is a significant factor in four, alcohol a major factor in six, and diet a significant factor in four. These factors are all lifestyle consumption habits that Americans can change if they want to.

Rather than spending money to find new medicines for heart disease and other dreadful ailments, government should put its money into encouraging people to have healthy diets (including large amounts of fresh vegetables and fruits) and to exercise regularly. In that way, Americans will live longer and healthier lives. But government does not work this way because then it would be attacking important special interests, such as the beef industry, the fast-food chains, and the people who own factory farms.

Fifth, medical researchers take far more credit than they deserve for the lives they save through animal research. These successes are unimportant compared to the benefits produced by other factors, such as improved sanitation, plenty of food, refrigeration, pasteurization, chlorination of water, and a high standard of living.

Sixth, when we switch our attention from animal research to the requirement of dissection in high school, college, and medical schools, we see that dissection is not necessary even for educational purposes. At the high school level, students often enroll in the biology class not because they are going to be biologists or doctors, but rather because they wish to fulfill a science requirement. Less than two percent of all students who dissect in schools and universities go on to work in the biological sciences. The argument that these students need to dissect animals as part of their education, therefore, makes little sense since they have no practical use for any knowledge gained from dissection. Each year, junior high and secondary school students dissect more than three million frogs and tens of thousands of cats, dogs, mice, rabbits, turtles, pigs, and other creatures, whose lives should be spared.

Even dissection for college and medical school classes can be eliminated. The existence of wonderful computer programs allows students to under- stand the anatomy and biology of animals. The computer images are so clear that budding scientists can get a better knowledge of the organs of animals from the computer than they can get from killing animals. If future doctors need practice in dissection, they can practice on cadavers, rather than on live animals. In their medical practices, most of them (other than veterinarians) will be treating humans rather than animals anyway.

Dissection is not only impractical, it is unethical, as well. It hardens young people to the pain and suffering that animals experience at the hands of human beings. Dissection fails to teach young people the importance of compassion and respect for human life. It is not surprising that people who are insensitive to the suffering of animals are often insensitive to the suffering of humans, as well.

★ ☆ ★ ☆ ★

Americans are a trusting people who have given far more respect to scientists than scientists deserve. Scientists deserve respect when they conduct their work in an ethical manner. They deserve blame, however, when they act unethically—as they do when they use animals for scientific purposes.

No. Animals play an essential role in science. To ban the use of animals in medical research and product testing would result in major setbacks to scientific inquiry and product safety. To prevent students from studying anatomy through the dissection of frogs and other animals in the classroom, moreover, would set back science education. Banning animal use in science education would make it almost impossible for the United States to keep its position as a leading center in medical research and health care.

Contrary to the emotional appeals of animal rightists, the use of animals for scientific purposes is highly ethical. In fact, not using animals in this way is highly unethical. Moreover, scientists who conduct animal research respect animals and treat them in a humane way. Finally, animal research is not only beneficial to humans, but to animals, as well.

Ethics. The animal rights position on the use of animals in science is itself unethical, and animal rightists rely on emotion rather than reason to appeal for public support. Ask yourself this question when you consider ethics: Suppose your mother, father, brother, or sister were dying. Would you regard it as ethical to let him or her die rather than permit the use of an animal for manufacturing a medicine or for a test that might allow your loved one to live?

That is the question that scientists have answered with a resounding "No" when they conduct research on animals. They fully understand that scientists have an ethical responsibility to treat animals humanely. That is to say, they believe in using animals for research, but scientists should not take part in foolish or unimportant experiments. Nor should they cause unnecessary pain. But they correctly assert that allowing humans to suffer when animal research can find cures for some of the worst diseases afflicting humankind is unethical. Most people in the United States and elsewhere applaud this position.

The ideas the animal rights movement is based on are examples of faulty ethical thinking. For example, to claim that speciesism is the same as racism and sexism makes no sense. Regardless of race or gender, human beings are morally and intellectually responsible for their behavior. When human beings discriminate because of race or gender, they are acting in an immoral manner.

But animals do not make ethical judgments. When a cat kills a canary, the cat is not acting immorally because a cat does not have the capacity to make moral judgments.

Nor is their any sound reasoning to the argument that we should be willing to give to animals the same consideration that we give to humans because children and the mentally ill are incapable of exercising moral judgment. First, children grow up and become adults, developing intellectual and moral capacities. Animals do not. Second, a human who is born or becomes mentally deficient is someone who has indeed suffered a great loss for which other human beings should be caring.

It is weird to hear animal rightists describing humans who believe in animal research as hypocrites. Hypocrites are those who pretend to be good and kind, but in fact are not. A hypocrite claims to support a certain principle, but does not actually follow that principle. For example, we expect members of the clergy to follow their religious vows and doctors to follow the standards of their profession. Are animal rightists themselves willing to live by their "ethical" convictions about the use of animals for scientific purposes?

Some no doubt do, but most do not. When they have diabetes, they use insulin—an animal product. If they refuse insulin, they die. Many people who support animal rights make certain that their children receive vaccinations, even when the vaccines are composed of animal products. When animal rightists need medical attention, they do not fail to get care that developed out of animal research. They do not want you to benefit from animal research, but they themselves are not willing to live by the consequences of their beliefs. And they have the nerve to criticize their adversaries as hypocrites.

Barbarism. Animal rights supporters play on emotion rather than reason when they describe gruesome examples of animal experimentation. A close look at the scientific uses of animals shows that the amount of pain that animals experience in science is minimal and that scientists use humane methods in animal research.

Diabetics must use insulin, an animal product, or they will die.

First, the number of animals used for scientific purposes is small. When we compare the number of animals people use in science with the number of animals people use in other ways, we get a broader view of the subject. According to the Office of Technology Assessment (OTA), a government unit that advised Congress for many years, the population of 260 million Americans keeps about 110 million dogs and cats as pets. Americans consume more than 5 billion animals each year as food. But researchers in biomedicine—medicine as it relates to all biological systems—use only between 17 and 22 million animals for their studies. One might never guess from the articles written on the subject that such a small percentage of animals are used by scientists.

Moreover, it is clear that the number of animals used in scientific research is dropping. According to Andrew N. Rowan at the Center for Animals and Public Policy at Tufts University, the use of laboratory animals worldwide has fallen by 50 percent between the late 1970s and the early 1990s. He says that a major reason for this drop was improvements in testing. Evidence from government agencies and private companies also show a drop in animal use for testing in the United States although exact figures are hard to check.

Second, laws require that animal research follow certain agreed-upon humane procedures. The AWA applies to all research labs—public or private, educational, or industry-based, whether or not they receive federal money—that use animals named by the U.S. Secretary of Agriculture. As of 1995, the law applies to cats, dogs, gerbils, guinea pigs, hamsters, marine mammals, nonhuman primates, and warm-blooded wild animals. Rats, mice, and birds are not covered, although the federal courts are considering including these animals.

The research facilities described in this law must register with the U.S. Department of Agriculture (USDA). They must meet the department's animal welfare regulations and standards. The facilities must report their activities to show that they are obeying the law. They must tell the department the number and type of animals they have used as well as the type of procedure (painful or painless). The USDA makes surprise inspections of the facilities.

The AWA puts limits on inflicting unnecessary pain on animals and sets requirements governing cage size, feeding and watering, lighting, ventilation, temperature, humidity, sanitation, and veterinary care for animals kept in laboratories. The law requires the establishment of animal care committees to supervise the conditions of the animal research. Each committee must include at least one veterinarian, one nonscientist, and one person not connected with the institution in which the experiment is to be conducted. The committee has the power to deny or suspend a research project involving animals if it has reason to believe that the project is not functioning according to the law.

The federal government has other laws and regulations governing the care of animals in scientific research. The Public Health Service (PHS) plays a role in this area. The PHS includes the Centers for Disease Control; the FDA; the Health Resources and Service Administration; the National Institutes of Health (NIH); the Substance Abuse and Mental Health Services Administration and units of the Office of the Assistant Secretary for Health in the Department of Health and Human Services. PHS policy requires that its units comply with the AWA.

Animal rightists blame the AWA because it does not include rodents, which make up 85 to 90 percent of the animals used in research. But what the animal rightists do not note is that PHS requires any facility receiving NIH money to obey the NIH *Guide for the Care and Use of Laboratory Animals.* The guide applies to all animals in the facility regardless of species. The federal government strongly enforces these rules. Other federal laws limit the use of animal experiments. Also, there are state and local laws and rules that apply to the use of animals in research.

Third, although animal rights supporters dramatize painful animal research, animal research is not necessarily painful. In fact, most animal research involves no pain. The use of painkilling anesthesia is standard in nearly all research involving operations. The figures are striking. According to a USDA report, 58 percent of the animals used in experiments in 1990 had no pain or suffering. Thirty-six percent were used in a manner requiring painkillers. And only six percent were involved in experiments in which animals experienced pain.

In the few studies in which pain itself is the subject of research, anesthesia is not used because scientists need to understand the point at which pain begins to be felt. In most research involving pain, scientists do not cause continuing pain to animals because such a system would tend to spoil the research.

Animal rightists make much of the pain inflicted through such tests as the Draize and the LD-50. But scientists take care to conduct these tests in a humane manner. For example, for the Draize test, known toxic chemicals or irritants are not placed in the rabbits' eyes. In the test the animals are first anesthetized—given anesthesia, which produces a loss of sensation—a fact that animal rightists never mention. And the chemical is put in the eye for no more than 15 minutes at which time it is flushed out of the eye with water. If signs of irritation appear while the test is going on, the test is ended and the eyes are flushed out with water. Most of the time, the animals receive medicine that allows them to feel the least possible discomfort. The pain-reducing drugs are held back only when they would interfere with the test result.

With respect to the LD-50, government agencies have changed their requirements. Federal agencies now advise that companies look again at older studies of safety and cosmetic ingredients. Moreover, federal agencies now allow for a "limit" test requiring 10 to 20 animals, rather than the 80 to 100 in the early LD-50 test.

One would think from the propaganda of animal rightists that researchers and businesses are anxious to use animals, lots of animals, for scientific purposes. But the animal rights movement did not become widely known until the 1980s. And even before then, researchers and business organizations were looking for alternatives to using animals for testing.

A driving force in the effort to find nonanimal research methods is the high cost of animal testing. Some studies have estimated the cost of using animals to test a single new substance is often more than $2 million. So the costs of evaluating the possible health hazards of 200,000 new substances each year are quite high. According to the OTA, in vitro tests are about one-tenth the cost of animal tests. They average $50,000 per product compared to $500,000 when animals are used.

Value of research. Scientists are willing to spend money for animal research and product testing because they are convinced of the value of these efforts. They fully understand that money for scientific research is limited. Scientists use animal research for several reasons.

First, nearly every major advance in biomedicine in the 20th century has involved the use of animals in research. Animal research has produced therapies and medical procedures, created lifesaving vaccines, and invented treatments for major illnesses. Here are just a few examples:

- Therapies and procedures: anesthesia, chemotherapy, insulin, antibiotics, tranquilizers, and organ transplants.

- Vaccines for polio, diphtheria, smallpox, tetanus, tuberculosis, cholera, measles, and yellow fever.

- Treatments for cancer, diabetes, jaundice, leprosy, arthritis, asthma, and epilepsy.

An example of the importance of animal research is the treatment of heart disease, which afflicts about 60 million Americans. Today, heart-disease victims can expect to live longer than people with that disease only 35 years ago when a heart attack at the age of 50 was nearly always fatal. For the gift of extra years, they can thank the scientists who used animal research to invent drugs to treat high blood pressure, developed surgery to open narrowed arteries to the heart, and created new passages around blocked places in these arteries (coronary bypasses).

The defeat of polio is one of many examples of the wonders of science in extending life expectancy and preventing great human suffering through the use of animal experimentation. Between 1948 and 1952, polio took the lives of more than 11,000 people in the United States. In addition, the disease partly or completely paralyzed nearly 200,000 Americans in this period. Today, youngsters take a vaccine that protects them from polio for a lifetime.

The animal rightists argue that the story of thalidomide (see page 29) shows that animal research is useless. The FDA, the federal agency responsible for assuring the safety of medical products, never approved thalidomide for sale in the United States. Dr. Frances Kelsey, an FDA medical officer, said that the safety information collected by European manufacturers in testing thalidomide was not sufficient. In developing the drug, the Europeans conducted no studies in teratology—the science that addresses the cause of birth defects. More extensive animal studies would have led European governments to reject thalidomide for sale to the public. If the story of thalidomide proves anything, it is the importance of animal research.

Scientists continue to use animals in medical research to find even new uses to end the diseases that have killed or hurt humans. Today, one of the worst illnesses is AIDS, which is causing death to large numbers of people around the world. C. Everett Koop, a former U.S. Surgeon General, expressed the views of most scientists when he said: "We'd be in absolute, utter darkness about AIDS if we hadn't done decades of basic research in animal retroviruses."

When animal rightists say that medicines work differently in animals from the way they work in humans, they are stating half-truths and are misleading the public. It is certainly true that animals are different from humans. One cannot assume that because an experi-

Through animal research, scientists created the vaccine for polio.

mental vaccination, medication, or procedure works for an animal, it will automatically work for a human being. But here the key word is "automatically." The important point is that some features of animals are quite similar to features of humans. So knowing how those animal features act under experimental conditions tells much about how comparable features might work for humans under similar conditions.

There are 250 diseases that are common to both humans and animals. Some treatments for diseases are the same for both humans and animals. Insulin, for example, is used for dogs and cats as well as for humans to control blood sugar levels. The polio vaccine given to humans is also used on chimpanzees to control outbreaks of polio.

Rodents are useful subjects for research in biomedicine because their body systems are similar to human body systems in many ways. In particular, rats are quite valuable to researchers. Most of the cellular and chemical machinery in a rat is identical or almost identical to that of humans. The structures and functions of the enzymes—the substances that speed up the chemical reactions of living cells—and cells are much the same. But rodents do not get all the diseases that humans do. So researchers use a variety of animals, including cats, dogs, rabbits, sheep, cattle, birds, and nonhuman primates in the search for answers to solve medical problems.

The case of cats is a good example of the importance of animals in research about humans. Although cats make up less than 0.5 percent of animals used in medical research, they have been enormously important in understanding health problems. Cancer—especially breast cancer—is common in cats. And cat tumors are more like human breast cancer than are those of a mouse or dog. Cats, therefore, have served as a useful model to develop and test new forms of therapy for this disease, which affects one woman in eight. Also, the most common fatal disease for domestic cats today is feline leukemia. And researchers are using knowledge from studying cats to develop early warning tests for human leukemia.

Surgical techniques for replacement of heart valves and pieces of larger arteries using artificial devices were first tested on dogs. Since hemophilia—a disease marked by excessive bleeding—in dogs is almost identical to that in humans, researchers study dogs to understand this disease. Researchers use chimpanzees in AIDS research because chimpanzees are the only primates that can be infected with strains of human immunodeficiency virus. However, no chimpanzees have yet developed an acquired immunodeficiency syndrome-like disease.

Animal research does not only benefit humans but it helps animals, as well. Benefits to animals from research in biomedicine using laboratory animals include:

- Pet vaccines for rabies, distemper, parvovirus, and infectious hepatitis.

- Treatment for animal parasites (heartworm, hookworm, and *Giardia*).

- Vaccines for livestock diseases (hog cholera, anthrax, tetanus, and blue tongue in sheep).

- Vitamin deficiency treatments (rickets, and white muscle disease in cattle).

- Pet cancer and heart disease treatments.

Without animal research, many animals would die. Animal rightists do no favors for animals when they support policies that will improve the health and save the lives of animals.

So much of the criticism of the use of animal research in medicine is based not on facts but on certain ideas about human life that are part of a way of thinking. The truth is that animal rightists make claims about the failure of science when their real plan is to protect animals no matter the cost in human life. Ingrid Newkirk, the national director of the leading animal rights group PETA, says that even if animal tests produced a cure for AIDS, "we'd be against it." And Chris DeRose, director of the animal rights organization Last Chance for Animals, says: "If the death of one rat cured all diseases, it wouldn't make any difference to me."

Second, the animal rights claim that the use of animal testing means that other kinds of research will not be used is false. Other kinds will continue to be used, but as supports, not substitutes, for animal testing.

It is true that animal research is not the only form of scientific research. And in vitro testing, clinical research, epidemiological studies, and computer modeling can and should be used for research. Developments in these nonanimal research techniques have resulted in fewer animals being used for scientific purposes than before the development of these techniques.

It is one thing to say that the amount of animal testing has declined. But it is simply false to say that animal testing is no longer needed. Cell cultures and computer models offer great insights into solving scientific problems. But they have vast limitations. For example, they cannot show how a new drug will affect the heart, nervous system, or a developing fetus (the unborn young).

When animal rightists claim that tests like the Draize and the LD-50 are not necessary, they are ignoring basic facts. The Draize test is used because no other test can provide the information that this test can. Rabbits' eyes are as sensitive as human eyes. FDA views the Draize eye irritancy test as the most meaningful and reliable way to evaluate the danger or safety of a substance introduced into or around the eye. Although the LD-50 test is used much less than it used to be, it is still used in rare instances, such as in examining the strength of highly toxic drugs. The FDA concludes that the use of in vitro tests alone does not necessarily prove that a substance is safe.

The fact that so many cosmetic companies no longer use animals in testing products is a result of animal-rights campaigns against the companies rather than scientific judgment. Still, cosmetic companies are legally responsible for the safety of the products that they manufacture. When many cosmetics companies claim that they do not use animal research to make their products, they mean that they do not now use ingredients tested on animals. But they use ingredients that were once tested on animals. They may also mean that the product was not tested on animals, but some of the ingredients were. Or the manufacturer did not conduct animal research but the supplier of the ingredients did. Or the manufacturer did the animal testing in another country. Even companies that pride themselves on selling cruelty-free products play this game.

When animal rightists recommend simple answers to product safety dangers, such as making more child-resistant packages, they are being ridiculous. Children can come into contact with poison or other harmful products after adults have opened a package and carelessly left it where children could reach it.

Third, the animal rightist claim that animal research duplicates existing research is yet another example of a half-truth. Of course, some research projects duplicate existing research. But medical research requires some duplication. Before the scientific community accepts a researcher's findings, it must be assured that the results can be reproduced. A limited amount of duplication is necessary to assure scientific truth. Often, however, charges about duplication are simply not true. Sometimes, nonscientists may think that scientists are duplicating research when in fact some variation exists in experiments. Scientists have to be careful in reaching conclusions when the facts are different—no matter how small the differences. The amount of duplication in scientific research is very small. Many researchers apply for government grants—money to pay for their research. But few manage to get government money for their purposes. Peer review committees, made up of experts who are very familiar with research studies, make the decisions about who gets grants. They do not support requests that will just be used to repeat existing research.

Fourth, the claim that government should focus on prevention rather than treatment is misleading. Even when people are careful to protect their health through diet and exercise, they get sick. We should not forget that many health problems are caused by factors that have nothing to do with prevention. Passengers in automobiles, boats, and airplanes become accident victims and sometimes receive severe internal injuries. Soldiers and ordinary citizens are gunned down, with survivors receiving brain or spine injuries. And some children are born with birth disorders. Animal research has been and continues to be important in dealing with these medical problems.

Even putting aside problems of health brought on by reasons that have nothing to do with the lifestyle of people who become sick or injured, we must note that so much of what we know is "healthy"—such as diet—comes from studies in which animals are used. Animal research is used in prevention studies for such areas as nutrition, vaccines, and behavioral studies. Without research on animals, progress in understanding the process of alcoholism or of the damage to body systems caused by alcoholism would come to a halt. Heavy government spending on prevention rather than treatment, therefore, would not change the need for animal research.

Fifth and finally, the use of animals in classes—whether at the high school, college, or medical school level—remains a vital part of the education of students. Dissection is important in biology classes at even the high school level. It provides a vital learning experience for the study of anatomy. Students get experience with real animals and body parts when they do actual dissections.

The knowledge about animal anatomy that students get from textbooks or computer programs is important to their education, to be sure. But students need to know not only book learning but hands-on skills, as well. Dissection allows students to learn about internal structures, interrelationships among tissues, location of organs, and the appearance and texture of tissues and organs. Dissection provides an understanding of an animal as a whole rather than as a collection of organ systems. Even when students do not major in biological sciences, the knowledge that they acquire from classes helps them understand public-policy issues of health and science research.

Scientists understand that they must care for animals and not abuse them. They correctly say that without animal research for medicine and product safety, knowledge and care of humans would be damaged beyond repair. Both humans and animals can only be hurt if animal research is ended. Animal rightists simply ignore the scientific evidence of the accomplishments of science.

Chapter 3
ANIMAL AGRICULTURE

Debate: Should Animal Agriculture Be Ended?

When the humorist Garrison Keillor was asked whether he ever thinks about the case for vegetarianism (the practice or belief in living on a diet consisting mostly of vegetable products, fruits, grains, and seeds, and sometimes dairy products), he said, "Between meals, mostly." Like most Americans, Keillor eats animal products. In fact, it would be difficult to think of Americans without the animal products that have become so much a part of the American meal: for example, meats such as hamburgers, hot dogs, ribs, chicken, and turkey; seafood, such as shrimp and tuna; and dairy goods, such as milk, butter, cheese, eggs, ice cream, and yogurt.

Take away animal products from American restaurants, and some of the great names associated with successful American restaurants, such as McDonald's, Kentucky Fried Chicken (KFC), and Burger King, might become little known—unless those restaurants changed their menus and served mostly nonanimal products such as salads, vegetables, fruits, and legumes. Those restaurants are not planning to make such a radical change, however.

If we look at the eating habits of the American people, we would be hard put to imagine that Americans would ever give up animal foods, since they eat so much of them. In 1993, the average American ate 112 pounds of red meat, 63 pounds of chicken and turkey, 15 pounds of fish and shellfish, 30 pounds of eggs, and 574 pounds of dairy products, according to the USDA.

Most Americans are carnivores, that is, flesh-eating mammals. To be exact, most Americans are omnivores, who eat both animal flesh and plant food. In spite of the popularity of food produced from animals, an increasing number of Americans are herbivores—plant-eating mammals.

People who limit their intake of animal products are vegetarians. Not all people who call themselves vegetarians give up all animal food products, however. The strictest vegetarians are vegans, who do not eat any animal products at all. Lacto-ovo vegetarians avoid meat,

The USDA recommends a variety of food products in their Food Guide Pyramid.

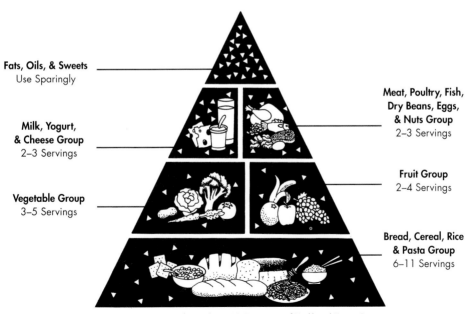

Food Guide Pyramid
A Guide to Daily Food Choices

Fats, Oils, & Sweets
Use Sparingly

Milk, Yogurt,
& Cheese Group
2–3 Servings

Vegetable Group
3–5 Servings

Meat, Poultry, Fish,
Dry Beans, Eggs,
& Nuts Group
2–3 Servings

Fruit Group
2–4 Servings

Bread, Cereal, Rice
& Pasta Group
6–11 Servings

Source: U.S. Department of Agriculture, U.S. Department of Health and Human Services

poultry, and fish, but do eat dairy products and eggs. (Lacto means milk; ovo means egg.) Lacto vegetarians avoid meat, fish, poultry and eggs—but eat dairy products. Dietitians—specialists in food quality and diet—refer to semi-vegetarians when they describe people who eat vegetarian food most of the time and occasionally eat fish or chicken and avoid red meat.

Some people have adopted vegetarian diets out of concern for their health. They feel that a diet made up of vegetables and fruits will keep them free of major illnesses, such as heart disease, cancer, and stroke. In this regard, Dr. Dean Ornish, a noted cardiologist (heart doctor), has shown that he can reverse heart disease in patients who, along with exercise and controlling stress, follow a strict vegetarian diet.

Some people become vegetarians for religious or philosophical reasons. In this regard, they believe that it is simply wrong for a human being to eat an animal since the animal is a living being capable of feeling emotion. These people do not approve of animal agriculture—the business of raising and selling animals mostly for food.

For its part, the animal agriculture industry has been forced to defend its practices in recent years. Such an effort is in sharp contrast to most of U.S. history when there was almost universal acceptance of animal agriculture.

DEBATED:

SHOULD ANIMAL AGRICULTURE BE ENDED?

Yes. Americans have been consuming animal products for so long that many of them think that they could not live on a vegetarian diet. But that idea is part of a thought pattern that needs to be changed. Americans continue to eat animal flesh because of habit and custom rather than physical need and ethical considerations.

Historically, ideas that are widely accepted lose their popular support when they become out of date for reasons of ethics, economics, health, or environment. Examples are many, but here are three that are well known: (1) Some cultures practiced human sacrifice as part of their religion. (2) People in many societies thought that they could not survive if slavery were abolished. And (3) many societies kept women in a lower social, economic, and legal position.

Human sacrifice, slavery, and sexism are no longer accepted practices in most modern societies. Another idea that needs to be condemned today is that human beings should breed, confine, scientifically manipulate, and slaughter animals to produce food for human use. The case against animal agriculture focuses on the nature of modern agriculture, health, and environment.

Modern agriculture. Farming today is big industry. Americans spent $593.8 billion for food in 1992. About half of that amount was for animal products. Each year, the U.S. livestock industry processes about 5 billion animals, largely cattle, pigs, poultry, and sheep.

Because of the money to be made from agriculture, farmers understand that they must operate efficiently. Unfortunately for the animals in their care, the need for efficiency means cruel treatment for animals. Some examples of cruel treatment are seen in the way animals are confined, raised, and abused.

Living conditions are grim for calves that are raised for veal.

A goal of agribusiness—the huge industry of agriculture—is to produce the most meat for the least cost, no matter how much brutal treatment is suffered by the animals. Because of costs, farmers force animals to live in confined areas. This confinement is as true of dairy and beef cattle feedlots as it is of closed chicken houses. Calves raised for veal live in single stalls, in which they are separated from other calves. Veal calves live in solitary confinement. Often, they do not have enough space to turn around. Most chickens are raised in battery cages—a series of connected cages—in which each chicken has a space about the size of a magazine cover—an area that is so small the bird has no room to stretch its wings.

The care of animals in animal agriculture is barbaric. Cattle are fed high-calorie diets, which can cause illness, such as indigestion. Techniques such as branding—the burning of a symbol into the flesh of an animal—and dehorning—the removal of the cattle's horns—are accepted practices of animal farming. Cattle are transported in crowded vehicles.

Overcrowded conditions produce horrible consequences. Some animals are so tightly confined that they kill or maim one another. The animals in confined spaces experience stress, boredom, and fear. Moreover, they easily spread disease.

Animals in agriculture endure the most terrifying torture in so many ways. Chickens are debeaked—a process that involves the placing of a hot iron to burn the tip of the chicken's beak. Debeaking is painful and sometimes causes the mouths of chickens to blister or to tear. Pigs have their tails cut off—a procedure that is known as docking. And pigs also have their ears notched for identification. Pigs are often raised on slatted floors, which cause discomfort to the animals.

Laying hens live in temperature-controlled battery cages placed next to each other in a series of rows. The rooms are always lit, a technique that results in the laying of more eggs. But it causes great discomfort to the hens because they are not able to sleep. Chickens are given drugs and antibiotics, mostly in their feed. The purpose is to promote growth and prevent disease.

In the name of productivity, animals are subjects of a system of bioengineering—the use of engineering in biology—gone crazy. In the early 1980s, for example, U.S. genetic engineers—scientists who work with genes, the basic physical units in cells that are passed on from birth from one generation to later generations—developed a cattle-growth hormone, known as bovine somatotropin (BST). An injection of this hormone in a cow results in an increase of 20 percent more milk than produced by nontreated cows. The hormone causes problems in some cows, including infection, spontaneous abortions, and even death.

In 1994, the FDA approved the sale of milk from cows treated with BST. In giving its approval, the FDA did not require special labeling of the contents of this milk. although BST adds hormones and antibiotics to milk and milk products. It also affects hamburger meat.

More genetic engineering is under development. Scientists predict that animals, such as cows and pigs, will be produced that are heavier than ever existed before. The fact that a genetic experiment sometimes produces a sick or malformed animal is of no humane or ethical importance to the experimenters.

Given the torture that animals experience in the agriculture business, one might wonder why the government does not prevent such inhumane practices. But farmers have much political power and are beyond the reach of the law. No federal law sets standards for the handling and care of animals on farms. Two federal laws deal with the humane transport and slaughter of livestock, however. State laws vary in applying anticruelty rules to farm animals.

Health. By U.S. law, all cigarette packages sold in the United States must contain a warning that cigarettes are dangerous to health. Until 1994, no warning about the health hazards of meat was placed on packages of meat sold in stores. That year, the USDA began to require labeling for the cooking of meat, however. If the USDA were really interested in protecting the health of the American people instead of serving the interests of farmers, it would order a label similar to the one the FDA requires on cigarettes.

Animal products can be dangerous to your health, as just one of many stories shows. In January 1993, three children died and more than 500 people became sick from eating contaminated meat prepared at a Jack in the Box restaurant in the state of Washington. It took such an incident to get the USDA to require safe-handling labels on packages of raw ground meat and poultry.

The cause of the contamination was E.coli infection, which is particularly harmful to children, older people, and people with a weak immune system—a network of cells that protects the body from harmful substances. Ground meat presents a particular danger because unless the meat is heated to 160° Fahrenheit (71° C), the heat does not reach the center.

One should not be surprised at the Jack in the Box incident. Many people get sick from eating animal products. According to the USDA, 40 percent of the chickens we buy are contaminated with salmonella, a bacterium that can poison people. Thousands of people get sick every year from food poisoning caused from mishandling of an animal product. Sometimes, people die from eating contaminated food. At other times they just get terribly sick. Sometimes, the incidents are reported, but often they are not.

Even when people do not get sick from eating animal products, they consume unhealthy substances. Animal products contain high concentrations of cholesterol—a substance that exists in the fat, tissue, and blood in all animals—and saturated fat—a type of animal or vegetable fat that increases the cholesterol level in humans. These are ingredients that have contributed significantly to the leading causes of death in the United States—heart disease, cancer, and stroke.

In addition, the animal products contain pesticides, antibiotics, and hormones that remain in the meat and are eaten by consumers. Some of the chemicals in these items cause cancer, allergic reactions, and anemia—a condition in which blood lacks enough red blood cells—in some people.

To maintain our health, we do not need to eat animal products to live long and healthy lives. Although meat and dairy products are rich in proteins, one can get enough proteins in a diet of grains, vegetables, fruits, and legumes. Too much protein can cause health problems, such as kidney disease and osteoporosis—a disease causing the loss of bone tissue mass.

Calcium is a part of milk. But calcium is also found in broccoli and green leafy vegetables. Besides, dairy products contain fat and cholesterol as well as lactose (milk sugar), ingredients that can damage health.

It is true that a vegetarian diet lacks vitamin B-12, which is necessary to maintain healthy blood. But B-12 deficiencies are rare. And one can take a B-12 supplement to obtain this necessary ingredient.

Environment. Animal agriculture is responsible for enormous environmental damage. It destroys land and pollutes air and water. Cattle need land for grazing. When cattle overgraze, they cause soil erosion and desertification —the process by which an area becomes a desert. Were it not for cattle raising, we would have more land on which to grow crops.

To produce a pound of meat requires 2,500 gallons of water. In comparison, to produce a pound of wheat requires only 25 pounds of water.

Meat is at the top of the list for foods in the amount of energy used per pound of product served. Energy is needed to process, package, transport, sell, store, and cook food. Pork needs more than 15 times as much energy to produce as fresh fruits and vegetables, according to Alan B. Durning, senior researcher at the Worldwatch Institute.

Animal agriculture has an impact on the environment.

Chicken production takes a heavy toll on the environment. One chicken processing plant may consume 100 million gallons of water in one day. Moreover, factory chicken production causes pollution in streams and groundwater.

One of the most serious examples of the damage that animal agriculture causes to the entire global community is the role it plays in causing the greenhouse effect. This effect occurs when gases, such as methane, carbon dioxide, nitrogen oxides, and ozone, rise into the atmosphere, thus slowing the rate at which heat escapes from the Earth. According to some scientists, the surface temperature of the Earth will rise because of these greenhouse gases, and will harm the environment. According to Earthsave, an environmental and health educational organization, 15 percent of the greenhouse gases that are overheating the atmosphere are caused by chemical farming methods now widely used around the world.

Animal agriculture harms the environmentally important rain forests. The great demand of the American people for beef products contributes to the loss of habitat—the natural environment of a life form that allows it to live and grow—not only in the United States but in other countries, as well. Because of the demand for beef hamburgers, the valuable rain forests in the Amazon basin in South America are being ruined to furnish the habitat for cattle raising. The result is the destruction of thousands of acres of rain forest, topsoil erosion, water pollution, and use of fossil fuels.

An important part of the environment is natural resources. Animal agriculture puts a terrible strain on natural resources. It uses one-third of the raw materials consumed for all purposes in the United States.

People suffering from poverty in the developing nations of the world pay a big price for the huge appetite that Americans have for animal products. According to the Council for Agricultural Science and Technology, an Iowa-based nonprofit research group, if all the grain used for livestock in the United States were eaten directly by humans, it would feed five times as many people as it does after being converted into meat, milk, and eggs. About one billion people on our planet are undernourished. Instead of using grain to feed livestock, we should be sending the grain to those people.

Aside from the ethical arguments about the cruelty of using animals for food, there are many other practical arguments. Not least of these is that animal agriculture causes serious injury to the health of humans. Moreover, it also produces deterioration of the scarce resources of our planet and causes damage to land, air, and water that can never be repaired. It helps continue the hunger that a billion people experience every day—particularly in poor nations.

No. Agriculture is one of the great success stories of the United States. Animal agriculture is an important part of the agriculture industry. The success of agriculture is one of the reasons why it has become a target of animal rightists. Today, most Americans have no direct experience with farm life. Less than 2 percent of the American people are farmers. Yet this small part of the workforce produces enough to feed not only the American people but many other people throughout the world.

The animal rights movement is made up mostly of people who live in cities. It is not surprising that they do not know very much about the part that animals play in agriculture. This ignorance leads animal rightists to make reckless, unfair charges. Farmers engaged in modern animal agriculture use humane methods to care for their animals. Moreover, animal products are healthy for humans to eat. And farmers protect the environment, rather than destroy it.

Modern agriculture. Animal farming today is a modern business activity based on the humane treatment of animals and the use of scientific knowledge for improved productivity. So successful is American agriculture that Americans spend the smallest share of their income on the food that they eat at home than do people in any other country.

Farmers take good care of their animals not only out of humane considerations but for economic reasons, as well. Farmers understand the effects of stress on animals. It increases deaths, reduces weight gains, lowers the immune (disease-resisting) function, and can have a harmful effect on reproduction. Rough handling of animals before slaughtering can damage the quality of the meat. No farmer would willingly mistreat livestock if he or she wants to make a profit. Farmers know that animals subjected to stress, abuse, or neglect do not produce as well as animals that are treated with care.

In fact, good animal care is made up of the very things that animal rightists claim are cruel. For example, animal rightists are against animals being confined. But animals kept in enclosed areas are safe from other animals who could harm them. The buildings in which animals are kept are well lighted and get plenty of fresh air. The enclosed areas permit conditions to be scientifically controlled. Animals housed in this way are less likely to get sick. They are also protected from bad weather. In most cases, the housing of farm animals, far from being cruel, is excellent and beneficial.

Animal rightists condemn the battery-cage system used to house chickens. The system is built to separate chickens from their droppings and to provide a clean and dust-free atmosphere. The battery-cage system allows each bird to get the right amount of food and water. Caging also allows for clean conditions. Eggs produced in this system are cleaner than eggs produced in a free-range system in which the chickens are allowed to move around over a large area rather than be confined to a small area.

The battery-cage system

The battery-cage system provides better treatment for chickens than existed earlier when farmers used their backyards to hold their hens. Life for backyard chickens was cruel and inhumane. Chickens faced disease, predators—animals that live by killing other animals for food—poisoning, and the attack of other chickens. The death rate of chickens early in the 20th century was as high as 40 percent. Today, it is about 10 percent.

Chickens are not the only species that live better lives in confinement than in open spaces. A farmer will put a sow (an adult female hog) in a stall when the animal is ready to give birth. The sow usually spends three to four weeks in the stall to make the process of giving birth easy, to make certain that it does not step on or roll over and crush her litter, and to allow veterinary care if necessary.

Dairy cows are milked in stalls, usually twice a day. This is the best way to use modern milking equipment. It is also helpful when giving medical treatment for an animal. After milking the cows, most farmers turn them out into larger pens.

When animal rightists target the treatment of certain animals, such as veal calves, as particularly cruel, they claim to know how animals feel because they believe that the feelings of animals are the same as those of humans. This attempt to see animals as having thoughts and feelings is known as anthropomorphism. But humans cannot know how animals feel about such matters as living in stalls, since animals cannot tell them in any understandable way.

The truth is that farmers treat veal calves with great care. The individual stalls allow each animal to get attention and controlled feeding. When a veal calf is placed in a stall, it becomes less likely to get hurt or become ill than is a calf that has contact with other calves.

Animal rightists, moreover, give an outdated description of housing arrangements for veal calves. In modern systems, veal calves can stand, lie down, see, touch, and react to other calves. Stalls are cleaned regularly, and the lighting is good. These conditions make sense because they contribute to productivity of the animal. Farmers do their best to keep their veal calves from developing anemia. Farmers check the blood level of veal calves regularly to prevent anemia because veal calves with this condition do not eat as much as healthy veal calves.

Farming techniques that sound so terrible to city people make much sense to farmers who understand the problem of raising animals. The docking of pigs' tails sounds cruel but is really humane. Pigs with docked tails are less likely to get sick than pigs without docked tails. Tail biting, moreover, occurs inside and outside of the pens.

Branding is necessary to show ownership since cattle stealing is a greater problem today than it was in the days of the Old West. Dehorned animals are easier to handle and suffer fewer bruises and less hide damage. And they become less likely to injure other animals and ranchers than animals that are not dehorned. Chickens are debeaked because they are often aggressive and can injure or kill other chickens. Moreover, beaks are trimmed, not removed.

Health. Animal products are healthy, as the leading government, health, and public interest organizations claim. Livestock products contain components that are essential to good health. These components include protein, calcium, iron, zinc, and vitamins A and B-12. Animal products contribute about three-quarters of the protein and one-third of the food energy in the American diet. In discussing nutrition, the Surgeon General recommends animal products, as do the U.S. Departments of Health and Human Services and the Department of Agriculture. The American Heart Association and the American Dietetic Association recommend lean meat in a diet.

Animal rights supporters are correct to complain about the dangers of saturated fat and cholesterol to health. But they attempt to equate animal products with saturated fat and cholesterol. And that is their error. If a person has an excessive diet of high-fat items, he or she is taking health risks. But any health-conscious person knows that it is wise not to have an overdose of high-fat foods. Moreover, many animal products are low in fat. Skinless chicken breast is a case in point. In fact, the healthy quality of chicken is one of the reasons that Americans are now eating more poultry. According to the USDA, annual consumption of chicken and turkey in the United States was 34 pounds per person in 1970. In 1980, it was 41 pounds. And in 1996, it was 64 pounds.

Animal rightists also attack milk as unhealthy. But milk is healthy. Moreover, many Americans now use skim milk, which contains no fat at all. People living in countries with the highest milk consumption have the longest life spans. Dr. Robert Kleinman, chairman of the American Academy of Pediatrics—the branch of medicine dealing with the care of children and the treatment of childhood diseases—notes: "There is no perfect food, but milk is a major source of a number of important nutrients."

Animal rights supporters point to the illness that the eating of animal foods has caused. But many of these cases involve inadequate cooking. All chicken is contaminated until cooked. Chickens must be cooked thoroughly to 180° Fahrenheit (82° C) to kill the bacteria.

Animal rightists object to the use of hormones and chemicals in the raising of animals. However, they do not give the public all the facts. Growth hormones are used in animal feeds, which are eaten by animals. But they are used in growing vegetable products, too. If hormones are dangerous to people who eat animal products, they are dangerous to those who eat plant products, too. But in either case, they are not dangerous when used under rules and inspection procedures set up by the government agencies responsible for overseeing food and health.

The chemicals used in the animal agriculture industry make for healthy products. Many eggs produced by chickens were contaminated by microbes from poultry diseases early in the 20th century. Thanks to pesticides and hormones, eggs are safer today than they were at that time.

And the huge uproar about BST lacks a basis in fact. The animal rightist attack on BST is typical of the animal rightist war on everything new. Animal rightists are afraid of changing the world even when science provides so many benefits to humans—and animals, too. The FDA, which is the organization responsible for evaluating drugs, approved the use of BST. Former FDA Commissioner David Kessler said, "Milk and meat from BST-treated cows [are] safe."

Animal rights supporters condemn practices that contribute to health safety. Antibiotics help animals avoid diseases. Growth drugs for cattle produce leaner beef.

Environment. Animal agriculture is a positive influence on the environment. The proper use of farm animals permits a conservation of resources within the total ecosystem. An ecosystem is a system of relationships among plants, animals, and the environment.

Animal rights supporters direct a good deal, probably most, of their criticism at cattle production. They falsely blame the cattle industry for soil erosion. Farmers understand the importance of conserving soil and are active in programs to prevent soil erosion.

Cattle production does not use excessive amounts of water. The drinking water for cattle ranges from 3 to 18 gallons per pound of beef sold to consumers. If irrigation water for feed crops is included, the amount of water per pound of beef sold to the consumer is higher. However, the amount of water use is much less than the 2,500 gallons claimed by animal rightists.

Agricultural production requires only 2.5 percent of the total energy used in the United States. Beef production accounts for only 0.5 percent of the energy used. More than 80 percent of the total energy involved in food production, processing (making the food ready for commercial sale, such as in canning and freezing), and preparation is used after the food leaves the farm. Animal rights supporters ignore the fact that plant-source food uses energy resources in processing, too. The amount of energy needed for beef processing is sometimes less than for plant processing.

Blaming the U.S. cattle industry for the destruction of the tropical forests is wrong, too. The United States imports no fresh beef from South America, where the tropical forest problem is particularly bad. The United States imports only cooked and canned beef—and only a very small amount at all. Moreover, less than 1 percent of U.S. beef comes from Central America. Tropical deforestation is caused by factors other than beef consumption.

Nor is the cattle industry responsible for global warming. Although methane is one of the greenhouse gases, it constitutes only 18 percent of those gases. Moreover, only 7 percent of the world methane production comes from cattle. U.S. cattle account for only 0.5 percent of world methane production and only 0.1 percent of all of any global warming effect.

Most land used for grazing is not suitable for growing food crops.

Carbon dioxide is a much more important factor in global warming. Automobile driving produces carbon dioxide. Dr. F. M. Byers, a professor in the College of Agriculture and Life Sciences at Texas A & M University, says that driving six miles each way to buy a hamburger would result in 100 times as much "greenhouse gas" as the methane generated in producing a hamburger.

The argument that land devoted to cattle reduces land for growing food crops is false. About 85 percent of the nation's grazing land is not suitable for farming or growing crops. Keeping this land from cattle grazing, therefore, would have no effect on plant production. The existence of ruminant livestock allows this important renewable land resource to have productive use.

The argument that the animal agriculture industry is responsible for the poverty of developing nations is also false. The grain used to feed livestock is feed grain, which is not suitable for human consumption. Moreover, the United States has no problem in producing grains. It could produce more if it chose to do so.

Finally, the reasons for poverty in the world are complex. But countries that were once poor have proven that they could develop strong economies and raise their standards of living, as the cases of South Korea and Taiwan show. Poverty exists in many countries because of ethnic conflict, civil war, and a lack of opportunity for investment—and not because some people in the western United States are raising cattle.

Animal agriculture is one of the great triumphs of the American economy. American farmers produce food efficiently and at low cost to consumers. They furnish the nation (and the world) with healthy food. And they are friends of the environment.

Chapter 4
HUNTING ANIMALS

Debate: Should Hunting Be Illegal?

Human beings have hunted animals in every culture and in every age. Cave paintings from prehistoric times show humans hunting animals. And written records contain many accounts of people who hunted.

Traditionally, people hunted for many reasons: for getting food, making clothes and other products, and taking part in sports and recreation. They also hunted to protect themselves against animals who might have killed them or damaged their property. Today, people hunt for a new reason: animal conservation—the preservation of a species so that it has sufficient resources to survive.

As a people, Americans have always hunted. Native Americans lived off the land and hunted. The early European settlers of North America hunted for food. The pioneers who moved westward hunted. Many U.S. presidents hunted; Jimmy Carter, George Bush, and Bill Clinton are recent cases in point.

Over the centuries hunters have used different kinds of systems and tools to kill animals because of both the characteristics of particular animals and the availability of new technologies. Early hunters employed rocks and rough traps. In time, hunters relied on bows and arrows, guns, and better traps.

About seven percent of the U.S. population hunts animals.

Today, hunters in the United States include not only private citizens but representatives from government agencies, as well. Arguing that the size of an animal population may be dangerous for environmental, economic, safety, or health reasons, government agents hunt—or allow private citizens to hunt—under certain conditions. For example, the USDA has a federal program, Animal Damage Control (ADC), for the purpose of killing mammals and birds considered to be pests. The targets of the ADC are animals that eat livestock or destroy crops—that is, animals such as coyotes, beavers, raccoons, skunks, bears, and mountain lions.

Although Americans hunt in every state, they may legally do so only according to federal and state laws. Government regulates the seasons in which hunters may kill certain kinds of animals and the number of animals that may be killed. Government may require hunters to pay a tax for the right to hunt. Some species whose numbers are so small that they face extinction may not legally be hunted in the United States. And in some cases, the United States has passed laws or signed treaties assuring that some species may not even be imported into the United States—whether the animals are dead or alive. Since some people hunt illegally for profit, fun, or other reasons, law-enforcement officials try to prevent such illegal actions by arresting poachers—illegal hunters.

Over the past few centuries, the percentage of the U.S. population that hunts has declined. In the late 18th century, when the United States became independent from Great Britain, most Americans were hunters. Today, about 18 million Americans hunt. This figure represents just 7 percent of the U.S. population. The decline in the percentage of the U.S. hunter population may be largely due to the changing character of the American economy. We have moved from a farming to an industrial culture. In 1880, half of all Americans lived on farms, and most of the farmers hunted. Today, less than 2 percent of the American people live on farms. Hunting is not part of the personal experience of most Americans today.

As hunting has become less of a part of the American experience, Americans have more and more become critics of people who hunt, whether for sport, food, or profit. Some critics condemn particular practices of hunters, such as the use of leghold traps or lead ammunition. Others direct their attention to hunters of certain kinds of animals, such as lions or deer. But the angriest critics of hunting are animal rightists. They object to the very principle of hunting by humans—although some animal rightists make an occasional exception to the rule.

DEBATED:

SHOULD HUNTING BE ILLEGAL?

Yes. An ethical person would like to think that human beings are capable of acting in ways that bring out the best qualities of people, such as compassion, reason, and understanding. Unfortunately, however, some people bring out the worst human qualities, such as brutality and insensitivity. When humans hunt and fish, they only show how deeply seated are the human emotions that produce acts of cruelty.

Hunting is barbaric, and it destroys the environment. The dangers blamed on animal behavior can be avoided if society adopts practical, humane alternatives to hunting.

Barbarism. The very act of hunting is inhumane since humans take joy in chasing and killing defenseless animals. We would not applaud humans who hunt other humans. Instead, we would condemn those killers. But our society has a double standard when it sees human violence against nonhuman animals as important.

Even if one does not accept the view that it is unethical to kill animals, one should at least be horrified by the methods hunters and trappers use for their executions. For example, the leghold trap contains a trigger that is connected to a powerful spring, which, in turn, is connected to a pair of powerful steel jaws. An animal is tempted to approach the trap by bait. When the animal steps on the trigger, the jaws clamp down on its leg. The animal is unable to move away and must remain in the trap until it dies or a trapper comes by to kill it. In a number of cases, the trapped animal chews off its leg or paw, a process that trappers refer to as "wring off."

The leghold trap captures any animals that come into contact with it. Somebody's pet can wander into the trap, as has often been the case.

So cruel is the leghold trap that many countries have banned its use. Some of these countries, such as Great Britain and Switzerland, are advanced

Hunters often use leghold traps.

industrial societies. But some countries that have banned it are developing nations, such as Bangladesh and Mozambique. Although most Americans are against the trap, the United States continues to permit its legal use.

Hunters using guns can be barbaric, too. Hunters often wound an animal instead of kill it. Many hunters do not bother tracking the wounded animals since it is easier to find other animals to kill. In this case, the wounded animal is left to suffer a lingering death.

Incidents of this kind are not surprising given the changing character of the hunting community. As hunting becomes more and more out of favor, the kind of people who do hunt lack the skills and traditions of the old hunters. Instead of tracking an animal that they have wounded for the purpose of putting it out of its pain, the new hunters just go after more animals. According to Joel Scrafford, a senior agent with the U.S. Fish and Wildlife Service in Montana, "We're seeing fewer skilled hunters who can cut a track and follow it all day." He added: "Now, we see too many four-wheel-drive, assault-rifle, gun-and-run, shoot anything yahoos who think they're Rambo."

Hunters seem to have no shame for the barbaric acts that they commit. Some of the most horrible hunts are nothing more than killing contests in which the hunters receive prizes for killing animals. In Hegins, Pennsylvania, on Labor Day every year, hunters shoot several thousand pigeons in what has become the largest one-day flyer shoot in the world. This event, which is witnessed by adults and children, shows great disrespect for living creatures.

Hunters regard themselves as sportsmen. But some of their activities are not really sportsmanlike. The "canned hunt" is a case in point. The canned hunt is any hunt in a human-constructed enclosure where the animal has no chance of escape. This area can be a small cage or a pasture ranging from a few acres to several thousand acres. Canned hunts exist in most states.

The cruelty that hunters inflict on animals may not alarm some people. But hunters commit cruel acts against other humans, too. Every year people suffer from hunting incidents. According to the Hunter Education Association, there were 107 fatal and 1,094 nonfatal hunting injuries in the United States (not including Alaska) in 1995. Hunters often like to blame animal rightists for being more concerned with animals than with humans. But they often ignore the dangers that hunting poses to innocent people.

Conservation. Hunters do much damage to our fragile planet. They are the killers of wildlife species. They destroyed the passenger pigeon by 1914. They nearly wiped out the buffalo, too. They have made leopards and other animals endangered species.

Hunters harm wildlife with their reckless use of equipment, as their choice of ammunition shows. When hunters use lead bullets, the spent shot falls into marshlands and waterways. This material produces lead poisoning in the marshes and fields where waterfowl feed. Lead poisoning kills as many as 1.5 to 3 million waterfowl each year. Because of the harm lead poisoning does to wildlife, hunters in many parts of the United States have been made to give up lead and use nontoxic steel loads instead. Many hunters objected to this requirement because of higher ammunition cost and because they were not used to this other kind of ammunition.

Lead poisoning caused by bullets containing lead has hurt not only waterfowl but other species, as well. These species include loons; Virginia, king, clapper, and sora rails; godwits; California gulls; coots; gallinules; scaled and bobwhite quail; ring-necked pheasants; mourning doves; prairie falcons; kestrels; red-tailed hawks; Andean condors; bald eagles; a California condor; and a whooping crane.

Hunters are anticonservationist in another important way. When people hunt, they go after the healthiest and strongest animals. These are just the ones that are best needed to preserve their species. In contrast, when nonhuman hunters seek their prey, they go after the kinds of animals that are easiest to attack. These are animals that are old or weak. They are just the ones that do little for the preservation of their species. Humans are a greater danger to a particular species than nonhuman predators.

One might hope that government conservation agencies, such as federal and state fish and wildlife agencies, would oppose hunters in their search for prey. What they do, however, is serve the interests of the hunters rather than the interests of environmental protection. These agencies help hunters by making the greatest possible number of animals available for their sport.

The mixture of hunting interest with public interest is shocking, as hunter influence in government wildlife agencies shows. Wayne Pacelle, national director of the Fund for Animals, uses one of what could be many examples when he notes: "Though only 1.4 percent of Californians hunt, there was never a nonhunting member of the five-member California Fish and Game Commission during the 1980s." He says that the same was true for Florida and for most other states.

Conservationists do not need hunters or wildlife agencies to manage wildlife. Nature will take care of it without that kind of "help." Deer, for example, would maintain correct numbers of their species without control by the government. In many areas of the United States, the deer population has remained stable without the help of government wildlife agencies.

In making their case for hunting, the hunting establishment uses scare tactics. They raise the issue of disease, particularly rabies, that can be spread by animals. Rabies is an infectious disease of warm-blooded animals that attacks the central nervous system. It is transmitted by the bite of infected animals. But rabies is a rare disease in America. An animal with the disease is not likely to attack a human. The argument of rabies danger to control animal population growth serves the interest of hunter and trapper prof-its rather than the interest of conservation of wildlife.

Alternatives. Some animals pose dangers to humans and their property. Humans have a right and a duty to protect themselves against those dangers. But humans exaggerate and misrepresent the dangers.

Hunters and trappers point to the financial burdens heaped on property owners from the "overpopulation" of certain species. It is no doubt true that some animals harm farm crops. But killing animals is not the answer to the problem. Many of the heavily trapped animals are plant-eating animals, such as beavers and muskrats, and they are no danger to the livestock of farmers. The predatory animals that are prized by trappers for the fur indus-try are small and are not dangerous to livestock. Mink, otters, bobcats, lynx, and foxes are examples. The bigger predators, such as wolves, cougars, and bears, are so small in number that they are not really a threat to livestock. And the coyotes are not as much of a threat to livestock as farmers claim. Moreover, humans do not need fur for clothing since so many synthetic and nonanimal materials are available. (See Chapter 6.)

Farmers still have to deal with predatory animals that endanger their live-stock. But they have many fine alternatives to killing animals. If farmers were humane, they would use these alternatives, such as building fences and setting humane traps. Fences would keep predatory animals away from

Box traps provide an alternative to leghold traps.

farmers' crops and livestock. Humane box traps that capture but do not kill animals are fine alternatives to the leghold traps that maim and kill. An animal captured in these traps can be released into the wild and would not be a threat to the farmers.

In areas where there are large numbers of deer, one can build overpasses. State road commissions can reduce driving speed limits. More importantly, they can see that such rules are obeyed. State agencies could cut back leaves and branches along the most dangerous roads. Then drivers could see well ahead in such areas.

To control the killing of sheep, farmers could use sheep guarding dogs. Friends of Animals, an animal protection organization, suggests other effective alternatives, such as noisemakers, light flashes, and strands of low-voltage electric wire.

One alternative to hunting is the use of birth-control vaccines. This system would reduce the number of animals born in a safe way. This procedure is used in zoos. It has also been used successfully with the famed wild-horse population on Assateague Island National Seashore off the Virginia coastline. And it could be used elsewhere, as well.

Another alternative is to relocate animals. It is more humane to remove animals from one area where they are overpopulated and take them to another area where they are underpopulated. Conservation money would be better spent in this way than in serving the needs of hunters.

Hunting is an abomination. People should not be misled by the foolish arguments of hunters and their supporters. Hunting is inhumane and hurts the environment. It is a violent way to solve the problems animals create for humans when those problems could be solved in a humane way.

No. Hunting is an honored practice for most people in all ages and in all cultures. People should hunt today for many of the same reasons that they have always hunted. Moreover, because of the change of society from agricultural to industrial, hunting has even more reasons for continuing as a practice than it used to be. Hunting should be seen as right and good because it is humane, helpful to the environment, and also practical.

Humane considerations. Like many other animals (lions, wolves, and cats), human beings are carnivores. As meat-eating animals, humans may hunt for food, just as other carnivores do.

When humans are rich, they do not need to hunt for themselves. They may go to the supermarket instead. When they are poor, however, they may have to do their own hunting and fishing. Some tribal people, such as the Aleuts in Alaska, depend upon hunting for survival. The same is true for tribal peoples in Canada, Greenland, Iceland, and other parts of the world. And poor people—whether tribal or not—often need to hunt to put food on their table. Poor people in such areas as Appalachia, the Ozarks, and the Cajun country of south Louisiana often depend upon hunting, fishing, and trapping for food and for income. Taking food and income away from poor people, as animal rightists would do if they had their way, can in no way be regarded as ethical behavior.

When animal rightists say hunting is cruel, they show an ignorance of life in nature. They are influenced more by the Disney picture of wildlife as shown in the cartoon *Bambi*. In this film, the fawn Bambi loses its mother to evil hunters but manages on its own, alongside animal friends, including a rabbit, a skunk, and an owl.

As with other animals in the wild, life for deer is far more cruel than the Disney film would have us believe. Nature treats deer harshly in many ways. Deer have many nonhuman animal enemies, that is, predators, who want to kill and eat them. If the deer survive their nonhuman animal enemies, they have the great task of living through dangerous weather. They may have a particularly cold, harsh winter. They may suffer from a lack of water because of little or no rain. Many deer suffer lingering, horrible deaths under these conditions.

During good seasons and conditions, deer experience difficult times because they produce more offspring than nature can provide for. Left to nature, the growing deer population will often devour all available plants. Unless humans step in to cut back the number of deer so that their habitat is able to feed and protect them, many deer will die. What is true for deer is also true for other animals, who face death from predators, weather conditions, and starvation.

Hunters and wildlife officials perform a humane act when they cull—that is, reduce an animal's population—to a level that allows many of its members to survive. The hunter is the friend of animals, not the enemy. Hunters and trappers are humane because they understand nature's cruelty.

To convince people with no experience in dealing with wildlife, animal rightists use photographs and descriptions of nature. When animal rightists show pictures of animals in traps, they appeal to emotion rather than reason. Most wildlife professionals approve of trapping as a means to control surplus animal population. Moreover, the number of incidents of animals chewing off their limbs is few.

The leghold trap is not the evil instrument of torture that animal rightists pretend it to be. Professional wildlife and conservation organizations use that trap, too. So do the U.S. Fish and Wildlife Service and state wildlife agencies. Such groups would not use the leghold trap if it were not a proper instrument for animal population control.

Trappers do not leave traps alone for long periods of time. They obey the laws of most areas that require traps to be checked every 24 to 36 hours. Trappers need to check traps often to avoid the loss of the trapped animal to a predator. Trappers care about pets, too. They take care to place traps in places where pets are not likely to go. Trappers use bait that does not attract dogs and cats.

Most hunters have respect for nature and for the animals that they kill. The idea that they are careless, insensitive, alcohol-ridden good-for-nothings is a false one. Most hunters do not leave a wounded animal stranded. Instead, they pursue the animal. To be sure, a few hunters are reckless and indifferent to the suffering of animals. But the existence of a few bad hunters is no more an argument for banning hunting than the existence of a few bad parents is an argument for banning fathers and mothers.

Animal rightists make much of the popular events in such hunts as the Labor Day shooting of birds in Hegins, Pennsylvania. But one of the purposes of this event is to collect money for civic projects, such as buying playground equipment for parks. Besides, the hunters kill only animals that serve no worthwhile purpose. At Hegins, hunters shoot wild pigeons that are pests and not homing pigeons.

Animal rightists are insensitive to the damage that animals cause humans, as the deer situation in Princeton, New Jersey, shows. In 1972, Princeton became the first New Jersey town to ban hunting with guns. Deer overpopulation became very serious. One result of this overpopulation was an increase in car accidents caused by the collision of cars with deer. In 1990, 200 deer died in Princeton from car accidents. This figure was higher than that for any other town in the state. Over the objections of animal rightists, Princeton has an annual bow-and-arrow hunt for deer. Robert Lund, a supervising biologist with the New Jersey Fish, Game, and Wildlife Department, recommended that Princeton hunt the deer. He put the matter plainly: "The issue is really simple.... Do you want to control the deer or not? If you do, the only real option is hunting. The only other significant agent of death is the car."

To be sure, hunting causes some human deaths and injuries. The number of such tragic accidents would be lower with more hunter-education programs. These programs teach principles of safety in hunting. But animal rightists object to hunter-education programs also.

Moreover, accidents happen in nearly every human activity, such as driving cars or taking part in engaging in sports, like baseball, football, and basketball. In the same year (1995) that hunting caused 107 fatal and 194 nonfatal accidents, recreational boating accidents caused 836 deaths and 4,965 reported injuries in the United States. Accidents are tragic facts of life. We hope they can be minimized with proper preventive techniques. However, they are not arguments for getting rid of the great joys of life.

Because of overpopulation, deer must find alternative sources of food, or face starvation.

Conservation. Animal rightists like to join popular movements in an attempt to hide their true purpose: to end all human use of animals for any purpose. Therefore, they link themselves with environmental groups. When they join forces with environmentalists, however, they are doing so only to get a temporary advantage for the cause of animal rights, not for the cause of environmentalism. They are not environmentalists. Their goal is to protect the lives of animals no matter what the cost to the environment. In this important way, they are antienvironmentalists.

The great dangers to individual species do not come from legitimate hunters. The hunters who are a threat to endangered species are poachers. They engage in illegal activities that hunting organizations oppose. A real threat to animal species comes mostly from the loss of habitat and from a lowering of the quality of the environment—factors that hunters are trying to limit.

Animal rightists use every charge to beat hunters into the ground, even when those charges are unfair. The accusation about ammunition is one example. Many hunters have switched from lead shot to nontoxic shot. They recognize the need to maintain waterfowl populations. Waterfowl biologists favor the use of only nontoxic shot for waterfowl hunting.

Hunters have always been in the lead of the conservation movement. They have supported government intervention in strengthening conservation efforts. In the 20th century, hunters have become the outstanding environmentalists. Hunters who were major figures in the conservation movement were John James Audubon, George Grinnell, and Aldo Leopold. Theodore Roosevelt, who was a celebrated hunter, founded the federal wildlife refuge system in 1903. Even the term conservation was coined by a hunter, Gifford Pinchot.

Both government agencies and private organizations committed to the protection of wildlife established wildlife preserves and public lands. In these places wildlife species are protected. Endangered or threatened species are helped to survive. And scientific management of wildlife is encouraged.

Today, hunters pay license fees and excise taxes on ammunition. Much of the money from these sources is used for purchasing habitat, including not only the home of animals but other supporting elements, such as food, shelter, water, and other animals.

Largely due to conservation efforts, the bison population in the United States has recovered significantly since the beginning of the 20th century.

In their zeal to blame hunters, animal rights groups claim that public lands are managed for the benefit of hunters. But that is not true. Only 12.5 percent of the animal species of birds and mammals found in the United States are legal game for recreational hunters. Much of the government tax money paid to manage wildlife species goes for birds and mammals that are not hunted.

The results of the conservation movement are impressive. Today, for example, the whitetail deer population numbers at more than 15 million animals from a low of possibly 300,000. Today, there are more than 1 million pronghorn antelope in the plains where once only 13,000 survived. Today, the bison population is more than 75,000 whereas in the first decade of the 20th century, less than a thousand bison lived in the American West.

Although hunters are interested in conservation, animal rightists are not. Animal rights supporters would rather see a species disappear than allow for any human intervention. And they do not care what impact overpopulation has on other forms of life, such as plants. Animal rights organizations challenged the culling of wild goats on San Clemente Island in spite of evidence that goats overgrazing the island caused the disappearance of 48 native species of flora and endangered six plant and animal species. Animal rightists also sued over the U.S. Fish and Wildlife Service's program to trap and kill nonnative red fox preying on endangered bird species, the least tern and the lightfooted clapper rail, at the Seal Beach Wildlife Refuge.

Hunters well understand that unless government and citizens acted to assure the preservation of habitat and species, the environment would not be hospitable to animals, let alone hunters or anyone else. They recognize that without hunters and trappers keeping wildlife to manageable limits, many species will overpopulate, destroy crops, and spread disease.

Finally, the problem of animals carrying disease is a real one. For example, animals do carry the tick producing Lyme disease, which is a threat to humans. And rabies remains a very real danger to the animal population.

Alternatives. Hunting—whether done by private individuals or government agencies—is a practical solution to the problems animals cause humans. The alternatives offered by animal rightists are not practical.

It is true that not all animals are meat eaters. But some animals are, and they are a danger to farmers' livestock. Animals that are plant eaters also endanger the crops of farmers.

The building of fences sounds like a good idea. But a fence is only good when it is strong and functioning. Many a fence is broken because of high winds, falling trees, or even ramming by animals. The amount of fencing that would be needed to keep animals enclosed would be so great that the cost of fences and fence upkeep would be impossibly high. So, too, would costs for clearing foliage and enforcing speed limits in rural areas.

Where would the money for fences and warning signals come from if hunting were banned? It certainly would not come from the money paid by hunter licenses and taxes, since hunting would be illegal. At a time when U.S. taxpayers are more than 5 trillion dollars in debt, it is unlikely that Americans will support raising taxes for such purposes.

Although scientists are developing birth-control drugs for animals, the use of birth control is impractical because of the huge number of animals involved. Some birth-control vaccines must be injected into animals. This takes a great deal of time and is very expensive. Other birth-control methods require repeated applications and may have some bad side effects. It is not possible to use animal birth control on any but a limited animal population.

Relocation is not a workable alternative for animals in overpopulated areas. The cost of moving animals is expensive. At a time of reduced government spending, no great popular support exists for such a measure. Even if it were popular, relocation often fails. Animals often move back to their familiar habitat. Some even travel great distances to reach home. Moreover, many animals die because they are unable to adjust to their new homes.

Humans are the caretakers of animals. They have a right to own and use animals for human benefit. But they must not abuse animals. Hunters are not abusive. Hunters play an important role in the conservation of animal species. Without hunters, the environment would be damaged and animals would experience great suffering.

Chapter 5
ANIMALS IN ENTERTAINMENT

Debate: Should Animals Be Released from Zoos and Aquariums and Returned to the Wild?

When the circus comes to town, people come to gaze at the playful actions of animals that move in the company of animal trainers, clowns, acrobats, and musicians. The United States is a country in which 80 percent of its people live in cities. They have little contact with animals except as pets. So the circus offers a chance for people to see live animals that they might not otherwise observe.

Children are particularly attracted to the circus acts, many of which feature animals doing funny stunts. For example, a lion jumps through a flaming hoop, and an elephant stands on its hind legs. The popular fascination with animals in circuses is not new to the world. Circuses existed in ancient civilizations of China, Egypt, and Rome.

Circuses are popular in the United States and serve as only one of the ways in which people use animals for entertainment. Other ways are rodeos, horse and dog races, horse-and-buggy rides, zoos, and aquariums.

Rodeos are particularly liked in the western United States, which is not surprising since American cowboys invented the contest in the 19th century. Rodeos show off cowboy skills and usually include three bucking events in which a contestant tries to ride a bull or horse under specified conditions. Rodeos also present timed events,

such as calf-roping, steer-wrestling, team-roping, and barrel-racing. Today, rodeos feature not only cowboys but cowgirls, as well. Moreover, even youngsters perform in rodeo events.

Horse racing and dog racing draw large crowds in America. Some horse races, such as the Kentucky Derby and the Preakness, are so well known that many Americans who otherwise pay no attention to horse races watch these events on television. Dog races are not as popular as horse races in the United States, but they still have enthusiastic followers. Both horse and dog racing are sports in which people legally gamble billions of dollars each year. Some special events, such as the Iditarod in Alaska, feature competitors running teams of dogs over the snow for days.

Some Americans use horses not for sports purposes but rather for light entertainment. The horse-and-buggy or carriage ride is a good example. Before the age of automobiles, Americans relied on horse-drawn vehicles as a means of transportation. Today, the carriage ride is a romantic reminder of an age gone by rather than a vehicle of moving from place to place.

Zoos and aquariums contain a greater variety of animals than any American could hope to see in one place. Some of the biggest zoos, like the San Diego Zoo in California and the Bronx Zoo in New York, collect species of animals that are found in different parts of the world. They show most of the animals in natural settings.

Although many zoos are large and established with some governmental money, still others are "roadside" zoos and have rather small collections of animals. Aquariums, such as the National Aquarium in Baltimore, feature big mammals such as whales and dolphins, as well as small exotic fish. Some zoos allow people to take rides on animals, and some aquariums have shows in which the dolphins jump out of the water and catch food.

Some kinds of animal entertainment, like cockfighting, involve so much bloodshed and injury to the animals that most states have made them illegal. And spectacles such as bullfighting—which ends usually when a matador (bullfighter) puts a sword through the head of the bull—are popular in Mexico and Spain but do not exist in the United States.

The love of animals as entertainment begins early in the life of an American child. Some of the most popular children's stories—*The Ugly Duckling* and *The Three Little Pigs*—feature animals. And the great film animator Walt Disney enchanted young and old alike with creations like Mickey Mouse and Donald Duck. In his lifetime Disney produced full-length films about animals, such as *Bambi*, which are still popular today. And even after Disney's death, the Disney studios continue to build on Americans' love of animal entertainment with such blockbuster films as *The Lion King*. Studios other than Disney have also filmed successful animal stories. One of these, *Free Willy*, is the story of the mistreatment and freeing of an orca whale. This was hugely popular in 1993.

Although most Americans enjoy watching animals, they differ about how they should enjoy them. As might be expected, people who benefit from animals in entertainment, such as animal trainers, performers, circus directors, and jockeys, praise the work that provides their income. But many others, with no direct financial gain, also support the use of animals in entertainment for reasons of belief rather than self-interest.

Animal rights supporters are among the strongest critics of animals as entertainment. They object strongly to the obviously brutal sports like cockfighting and bullfighting. But they are also against all other types of human use of animals in entertainment, such as circuses, rodeos, horse and dog races, horse-and-buggy rides, zoos, and aquariums. They argue that humans should enjoy animals—but only at a distance.

Beginning with the belief that humans have no more right to own or use an animal than they have to own or use another human being, they object to the display of animals under captive conditions. We can understand their arguments as well as the opposition to their arguments from a debate about zoos and aquariums.

Roadside zoos lack the professional staff support and facilities that larger zoos have.

DEBATED:

SHOULD ANIMALS BE RELEASED FROM ZOOS AND AQUARIUMS AND RETURNED TO THE WILD?

Yes. The business interests that use animals as a means to make money know how to play on the emotions of people since animal entertainment causes human feelings of joy, amusement, competition, and triumph. But even if we leave aside the ethical argument that humans have no more right to own or use an animal than they have to own or use another human being, these selfish users of animals do more harm than good.

The case of the zoo and aquarium is a good example. These institutions, although popular, are cruel to animals, undermine conservation, and give the wrong information about animals as a means of education.

Cruelty. Zoos and aquariums may appear to be places that offer enchantment. But in fact, they are institutions that cause great cruelty to animals.

First, zoos and aquariums are no better than prisons. Even the best zoological institutions with the finest facilities are prisons. No talk about the fine modern facilities can change this judgment. Zoos, like prisons, pen up living beings. In the one case, they limit the freedom of humans. In the other, they limit the freedom of nonhuman animals.

In numbers, most zoos are small, roadside zoos rather than the big, established institutions, like the National Zoo in Washington, D.C., or the San Diego Zoo in California. In the United States, roadside zoos number more than 1,000. But the American Zoo and Aquarium Association (AZA), the official professional association, has only 175 accredited institutional members (as of April 1997). AZA zoos are professionally run, unlike many of the roadside zoos. Lacking the facilities and professional support that the established zoos possess, roadside zoos neglect and mistreat the animals in their menagerie (collection).

Second, one need only look at animals in zoos to understand how hard life must be for them. Boredom is a constant feature of life for zoo-imprisoned animals as people can see from the frequent pacing of animals back and forth and swaying from side to side. Animal protectionists have found examples of zoo animals becoming so bored and so confused from their being penned up that they inflict pain on themselves.

Zoos and aquariums have attempted to replace the small cages that existed for so many years with a so-called natural habitat, or ecosystem as some defenders of zoos call it. But they cannot come close to reproducing a natural environment for most animals. A tiger in the wild travels miles in one day to hunt for food. In captivity, even under the best of circumstances, its moving space is measured in terms of square feet or square yards. Wild bottlenose dolphins travel up to 100 miles (160 km) a day and can dive hundreds of feet below the surface. Marine parks and oceanariums confine dolphins to cramped concrete tanks. Federal rules set up a minimum tank size of 24 feet (7 m) in diameter, or twice the body length (whichever is greater) and 6 feet (2 m) deep per dolphin.

To the outside observer, the natural surroundings of animals at a zoo may look "real." When you put a polar bear in a zoo in Atlanta, San Diego, or some other city with a temperate or hot climate, you can believe that the polar bear thinks it is home in the Arctic. But the polar bear can tell the difference between the real world and the fake world.

Third, many animals suffer in the hunt to capture them in their natural habitat. Marine mammals particularly are subjected to stressful hunts. When they are captured, they often become ill, and many die. And animals suffer, too, when they are moved from their natural habitat or even from one to another. At times, the creatures die during the move.

Fourth, zoos move animals around to serve their own interests rather than the needs of the animals for which they are supposed to care. Sometimes a zoo will decide to ship an animal to another zoo in the hope that it will find a mate there. When an animal leaves its home in this way, it gives up the social environment of friendly animals and becomes confused and unhappy. The transported animal becomes uncertain and sad because the physical surroundings of the two zoos are usually not alike. An animal also becomes disoriented from leaving the wild. For example, dolphins are incredibly social animals that live in family groups. But they are torn from their families when captured for aquariums.

Fifth, a great problem for zoological institutions is that animals imprisoned there produce more offspring than the institutions can care for. The zoos cannot kill healthy animals because killing animals would hurt their image as a friend of animals. So the zoos must get rid of the animals in some other way. They either sell them to zoos or to dealers in animals. Once the zoos transfer animals, however, they have no control over what happens to them.

Some zoos have even sold animals directly to the owners of hunting ranches. Some hunting ranches in the United States allow hunters to hunt exotic game. For a fee, the hunter can kill an animal and use it as a trophy of his or her hunting ability—like a deer's head over a fireplace. In some countries zoos kill their extra animals. Or they sell them to laboratories for animal testing, or to circuses for performing before the public. Or worse yet, zoos sell them to restaurants where they will be killed and eaten.

Blame for the fate of these animals does not really belong to the dealers because they did not create the problem of surplus animal population. Blame goes to the zoos, which did create the problem. For the animals who die from a hunter's bullet or arrow, however, it does not matter who is at fault.

Conservation. Zoological institutions make much of their role in conservation of endangered species. But the claims are mostly propaganda rather than facts.

First, zoos and aquariums save only a small percentage of endangered species. According to Andrew Dickson of the World Society for the Protection of Animals, an animal-protection organization, only 2 percent of endangered species are being bred in zoos. And only one in 20 of the world's zoos can claim to be doing anything at all for conservation. Most animals in zoos are bred and shown in zoos to attract visiting crowds rather than to preserve endangered species.

Second, some species have a better chance to survive in the wild than they do in captivity. Wild pandas die in captivity faster than they reproduce. When pandas are in zoos for a long period, their cubs rarely survive. Ling-Ling, the famous panda that was a gift to the Washington National Zoo from the People's Republic of China in 1972, had five cubs with her mate Hsing-Hsing. All of the cubs died.

According to Dr. John Grandy of the Humane Society of the United States (HSUS), the four small whale species currently held in captivity (the killer whale, the false killer whale, the beluga, and the pilot whale) suffer unnatu-

Giant pandas Hsing-Hsing (left) and Ling-Ling mated while in captivity at the Washington National Zoo, but none of their offspring survived.

rally high death rates, shorter life spans, and low birthrates in captivity compared to the same animals observed in the wild. He adds that the average life span in captivity for all four species combined (assuming a capture age of three years, which is typical for these species) is eight years. In the wild, he says, the average life span is 25 to 35 years.

Third, we question whether species preservation through the use of zoos is a good idea. If human beings are going to take over the habitats of animals so that certain species can no longer survive except for the fortunate few who are rescued by a zoo, it is probably a better idea to allow that species to become extinct. From an ethical point of view, we should be guided by the belief that all living animals have a right to freedom. They should be allowed to live out their lives in the natural environment. Species should at least be able to die with dignity.

Fourth, the best way to strengthen conservation of endangered species is to control human behavior rather than animal behavior. One of the great threats to animals is the loss of habitat brought on by a growing human population, deforestation, overdevelopment, and pollution of air, water, and land.

When zoos remove animals from their natural habitat, they undermine the strength of arguments for conservation. When an endangered species is taken from its natural environment, greedy developers say that more land can be cultivated for human use because the endangered species has been saved. If an endangered species is so removed and the land on which it depends is commercially developed, zoos will not be able to release the captive species into the wild because its natural environment would have been destroyed.

World human population increases by 250,000 people every day. This development places increasing pressure on the world's food resources. By 2050, human population is expected to be 9 to 12 billion, up from 5.8 billion in 1995. Tropical rain forests decrease by 100 acres per minute. This process reduces the habitat for thousands of species. The decline in habitat caused by overdevelopment is responsible for the extinction or near-extinction of some species of animals. And pollution created by industrial wastes and pesticides kills animals, too.

Animal extinction is occurring at an increasing rate. According to the AZA, from the time of Christ until 1800, one animal species vanished every 55 years. From 1800 through 1900, one species disappeared each 18 months. And from 1900 until today, one species is lost every 12 months. Moreover, forms of life other than animal forms are becoming extinct at a similar rate.

If we really want to preserve endangered species, we have to get serious about enforcing the laws and international agreements for protecting these species. Poachers in China have made the panda an endangered species that may be extinct by the year 2025, according to wildlife authorities. And the authorities also note that poachers in India made the Bengal tigers an endangered species, which may become extinct before 1999.

Education. Everybody who loves animals favors the education of the public about animals. But zoos do not educate well, and most importantly, they teach the wrong lessons to people.

Most people who go to zoos and aquariums are not interested in education as such. They go there for fun. They enjoy seeing the popular species, such as pandas and elephants in the zoo and whales and dolphins in the aquarium. But what do the people learn other than the few facts placed near the area where the animals are held?

It is true that zoological institutions provide lectures and demonstrations to people of all ages. Today, however, one can learn more from National Geographic and other nature films about different species than one can get from visits to zoo exhibits. These films present detailed pictures of species as well as the comments of researchers who have great knowledge of the biology and behavior of animals in the wild.

Educators should support practices like those of The Cousteau Society's Ocean Park in Paris. It is a museum with no live animals. It has video displays and films of the sea world. It even has a life-size model of a 90-foot (27-m) blue whale through which visitors can walk.

Finally, zoos and aquariums teach the wrong lessons about animals. The message that they give to the public is that it is perfectly moral for a human to control an animal rather than treat the animal as a living being. This is the message of speciesism, a belief that is basically immoral.

Americans would do well to join the campaign to expose the tyranny of institutions like zoos and aquariums. These institutions do dreadful harm to animals, and they undermine respect for the value of life.

No. It is not surprising that every year, more than 115 million Americans visit professionally run zoos, aquariums, oceanariums, and wildlife parks. In fact, more people go to these places than go to all big league football, baseball, and hockey games combined.

Some people go to zoos and aquariums for entertainment. But many people go there because they know that these institutions treat animals well, promote conservation, and educate the public about animal behavior and the preservation of animal species.

Cruelty. Zoos and aquariums make life comfortable, healthy, and pleasant for the animals in their care. Animal rightist accusations of cruelty to animals are filled with largely inaccurate and sensational information. The accusations are unfair to the zoological institutions and to the men and women who devote their lives to caring for animals there.

First, to compare zoos and aquariums to prisons is a false analogy because the comparison implies that the animals are in some way being punished. In fact, they are being pampered. Zoos provide nutritious food and an abundant amount of water. When temperatures get too hot or too cold, the animals move from the outdoors to a comfortable climate-controlled environment. When the animals are sick, zoologists and veterinarians come to their aid. Even when the animals are not sick, the caretakers furnish medicines and vaccinations to protect the animals from the kinds of illnesses they would likely get in the wild.

When animal rightists complain about the imprisonment of animals in zoos and aquariums, they give an image of a stable, quiet, happy, and peaceful environment that the creatures would experience in the wild where they would roam far and free. The image does not reflect reality. A forest animal will always stay in the forest and even when it remains there, it must be careful not to wander into areas populated by its predators. An animal in a zoo lives in a place that keeps it safe from a natural predator. No hunters or poachers threaten animals in the zoos and aquariums. And animals in the wild often have to migrate to avoid water or food shortages. It is no wonder that the life expectancy of animals is higher in captivity than it is in the wild.

If we want to be cruel to animals, we would follow the recommendations of animal rightists by releasing the animals held in zoos and aquariums to the wild. If animal rightists achieve their goal of closing zoos and aquariums, they would be causing the death of the very creatures they want to help. Today, more than 80 percent of mammals displayed in North American zoological institutions are captive born, and 50 percent of these are offspring of captive-born parents. Since most of the animals in zoos and aquariums are born in captivity, they would not even know how to survive in the wild.

Moreover, it is wrong to say that the roadside zoos are the same as the AZA zoos. Although roadside zoos are large in number, the bigger established zoos play the major part in showing animals to the public. And both the large and the roadside zoos must meet strict federal and state government laws and regulations dealing with treatment of animals.

Second, animal life is not boring or confining in zoos. Animals in zoos have room to move about. Gone are the days when zoos stacked up animals in small cages according to species. Over the past few decades, zoos have modernized their facilities. They have reproduced the animal's natural habitat as much as possible. They try to make their environment like the ecosystem and geographic area from which its species came. Today, animals move about in an environment of trees, grass, ponds, and rocks.

Third, when animals are moved from place to place, the caretakers take careful measures to assure the safe movement of the animals. Zoos and aquariums have improved their techniques for capturing or transporting animals safely. When one reads about an animal death in captivity, the animal rights activists present this case as evidence of cruelty. In reality the case is an exception to good supervision.

Fourth, zoos pay great attention to the social and psychological needs of the animals in their care. That is the reason why they do not isolate animals in separate cages. Instead, as mentioned, they place animals in a friendly social environment with animals that their species find compatible. Most animals that are moved to new places show no signs of being confused in their new homes.

An aquarium employee prepares to move a dolphin to a new home.

Fifth, it is unfair to criticize zoological institutions for creating a problem of surplus animals. The problem of surplus animal population is greater in the wild than it is in zoos. Animals in the wild overpopulate so much that they often destroy the food sources they need to live.

In moving surplus animals, AZA has a Code of Professional Ethics, which forbids the selling of zoo animals at auction or to hunting ranches. Dealers who buy animals from AZA zoos must sign agreements that they are obeying the code. The AZA punishes its members who do not obey the code. The cases of violations are exceptions to a practice that is usually followed. Violations of the code are not usual.

Conservation. Zoos and aquariums are major conservation institutions that promote research and assist in the preservation of endangered species. Zoos and aquariums pioneered in developing breeding programs for many endangered species.

First, zoos and aquariums have been successful in returning endangered species into the wild. The Phoenix Zoo successfully reintroduced the Arabian oryx, which is similar to an antelope, to the deserts of Oman and Jordan. The Point Defiance Zoo in Tacoma, Washington, and the Wild Canid Survival Center near St. Louis have reintroduced red wolves to a North Carolina wildlife refuge. Without the efforts of zoos in preserving endangered species, the Mongolian wild horse, golden lion tamarin, European bison, and Père David's deer, which have been reintroduced into areas from which their species came, would have disappeared from our planet.

One of the most successful efforts at protecting an endangered species is the attempt to preserve the California condor, the largest land bird in North America. Federal officials decided to breed the condors in captivity because the species faced extinction. The San Diego Wild Animal Park and the Los Angeles Zoo were successful in raising the condors and reintroduced a few of them into the wild.

It is certainly true that zoos will not be able to keep all species from becoming extinct. But zoological institutions have had some successes, and they are going to have even more because of new ideas and methods in breeding programs. AZA established a Species Survival Program (SSP) in the early 1980s to coordinate breeding efforts by zoological institutions. The organization connected its program to efforts of two international groups. By 1997, the AZA managed SSPs for over 120 endangered species.

After being bred successfully in captivity, the California condor was reintroduced into the wild.

To prevent animal inbreeding (the mating of closely related animals), each program kept records of its animals, including information on sex, parentage, place of birth, and location. Inbreeding provides an offspring with identical genes. It often results in problems in strength, size, and reproductive ability of offspring.

Zoos are so deeply involved in preserving and breeding endangered species that their officials properly refer to themselves as modern arks. In making this reference, they call to mind the biblical Noah, who took on board his ark two members of each species and, according to the Old Testament, saved the creatures from the Great Flood.

Second, although some animal species may live longer in the wild than in captivity, most do not. From 40 percent to 90 percent of all young born of most species in the wild are killed, starve to death, or die of disease, accident, or other causes before they are old enough to reproduce. Zoos and aquariums cut way back on this loss because of the care they give to the animals.

Third, the alternative to ending breeding programs of endangered species is to do nothing. Animal rights supporters are willing to accept the consequences of the disappearance of animal species rather than permit humans to preserve the creatures in zoos and aquariums. Once these endangered animals are gone, however, nothing can bring them back. If we care about animals, we should try to keep as many species as possible until such time as humans are able to control the forces that have been so harmful to animals.

Fourth, no one would deny that human beings are responsible for much of the loss of wildlife species to the world. And many conservationists agree that humans can do much to control the forces that threaten the environment. But those developments are not enough to deal with the problem of species extinction.

It will take time to change people's ideas about the environment. The development of environmental protection laws and international agreements protecting endangered species show the growing awareness across national boundaries of the fragility of our planet. Zoos and aquariums have played an important role in educating the public about species survival and have contributed to the changing attitudes.

In addition, scientists are inventing new technologies to improve the environmental quality of our planet. It is quite possible that so long as some endangered species can be saved because of zoological institutions, these species will be reintroduced into the wild at a time when the wild will be less dangerous for them.

Moreover, animal rightists are wrong to argue that once an endangered species is removed from its natural habitat, conservationists weaken their arguments. So long as a population of an endangered species exists, whether in the wild or in captivity, the chances for preserving the habitat are strengthened. If the California condor had become extinct, conservationists would have had no good argument for saving its habitat. But now that the California condor population is growing, the arguments for commercial development of condor habitat are weak.

Education. Zoos and aquariums are important educational resources for the general public as well as for students at all levels. They are also important resources of zoologists and veterinarians and others who either conduct research or tend to the medical care of animals.

At a zoo or aquarium, Americans have opportunities to see the world of nature in its great diversity. Elephants and tigers from India, giraffes from Tanzania, lions from Kenya, pandas from China, monkeys from Rwanda, and hippopotamuses from Africa are among a zoo's most popular attractions. Seals from Alaska and whales from the North Atlantic draw crowds of admirers to aquariums.

In the late 20th century, zoos and aquariums are more than showcases for animals. They are educational institutions, as well. Modern zoos and aquariums invite schoolchildren to their facilities and present lectures about the animals in their care. Each year, eight million schoolchildren visit zoos and aquariums as part of their school year studies. And AZA institutions provide training to 25,000 teachers.

Zoos and aquariums are institutions of higher learning, too. AZA institutions hold international training programs for zoologists and wildlife managers. It is no wonder that researchers first learned about important matters of

Each year, eight million schoolchildren visit zoos and aquariums as part of their school year studies.

animal biology, health, and behavior from studies of animals in captivity rather than from expeditions in the wild. Some examples include gestation (pregnancy) and incubation (the time needed to hatch or develop) periods, development of the young, and life expectancy. Other examples are tranquilizers for animals and analyses of chromosomes—the structures in cells that carry genes. The knowledge gained from research on animals in captivity will help preserve animals in the wild.

Students and nonstudents alike can learn much about animals from just reading the signs and looking at the exhibits at zoos and aquariums. Visitors often learn about the biology of the animal and the location of its species. They also learn about environmental threats that the species encounters. A Roper poll shows that 86 percent of the American people believe that they are more likely to be in favor of environmental conservation after a visit to a marine park or a zoo than they would be if they had not.

Zoos and aquariums are a national treasure in the United States. They make Americans aware of the wonders of nature. They protect animals, and they serve as a modern Noah's ark for endangered animal species.

Chapter 6
FURRY ANIMALS

Debate: Should We Be Ashamed to Wear Fur?

As passengers walked from their planes to the terminal at Washington National Airport a few days before Christmas in 1991, they were met by animal rights activists wearing fur coats spattered with red paint. When the activists spotted someone wearing a fur coat, they scolded that person. Confronting the fur-clad passenger, the demonstrators held up pictures of a caged fox, bearing the caption: "We'd like you to meet someone who used to wear fur." And one of them said: "Nice coat. How'd you get the blood out?"

The passengers were not amused and tried to avoid their unwelcome critics. Most of them responded to the unpleasant condemnation with obscene remarks. These remarks did not bother Dan Mathews, director of PETA's antifur campaign. "If people are still wearing fur coats after all the years of our movement, they're not ignorant," he said. "They're arrogant, so they deserve to be confronted more aggressively."

The scene at Washington National Airport is one of the many examples of protest that animal rights activists have conducted against the human use of fur. As mentioned in Chapter 1, every year on the day after Thanksgiving, demonstrators gather outside of fur salons and department stores that sell furs and peacefully protest the sale of furs. For example, on Friday, November 25, 1994, antifur demonstrators picketed stores selling furs in about a dozen cities, including Atlanta, Chicago, Dallas, Los Angeles, Miami, New York, St. Paul, and Washington, D.C. Not all the demonstrators were peaceful, however, and the police arrested about 40 of them.

More militant activists have not been content with legal means of protest. These extremists have occupied the offices of clothing designers, such as Kurt Lagerfeld, who use furs in their collections. A small segment of the animal rights movement goes even further in illegal activity by damaging fur garments in stores and in cloak-rooms or by squirting red paint from spray cans on them, or by cutting them. Some activists even set fires in stores that sell furs or in companies that distribute furs to stores.

Most animal rights supporters do not take part in violent acts. Although they vary in the methods that they use to protest, they are as strongly opposed to using furs in clothing as health supporters are about smoking. They have enlisted some of the top personalities in entertainment and fashion, such as Candice Bergen, Mary Tyler Moore, and Cindy Crawford, to dramatize the issue. They have succeeded in winning a greater measure of popular support on the issue of furs than they have in other areas of the animal-rights program, such as getting people to become vegetarians or to oppose the scientific use of animals in medical research. Some stores in the United States and abroad no longer sell furs. Sears Roebuck in the United States and the famous department store Harrod's in Great Britain have given up their fur collections. And many fur stores have gone out of business.

To judge the issue of wearing fur, some basic facts about fur need to be understood. Furs are animal hides that are tanned leaving the hair on. Furs are used in many ways, but most notably in clothing. In the United States, 90 percent of fur coats are worn by women. Furs today are produced mostly in Scandinavia, the independent countries that used be part of the Soviet Union, China, the Netherlands, the United States, and Canada. According to the Fur Farm Animal

Welfare Coalition, the national organization that oversees humane care standards for American mink and fox farms, the United States has 10 percent, and Canada 3 percent, of world pelt production. A pelt is the skin of an animal with the fur or hair still on it.

Furs are gathered from animals primarily in two ways: by trapping, which goes on in most states, and by fur farming. We have already discussed trapping in Chapter 4 on hunting, so we will focus our attention here on fur farming.

In the United States, the fur farm industry is found almost entirely in the northern states. Wisconsin, Minnesota, and Utah have the largest fur farming industries. In Canada, Ontario and Quebec contain the most fur farms while the Atlantic Provinces have the largest number of fox farms.

In North America, animals farmed for furs include mink, fox, lynx, bobcat, rabbit, and chinchilla. Mink make up about 90 percent of all ranched furbearer animals in the United States. Most of the fur farms are family owned, although they vary in the number of animals that they raise.

Demonstrators gather the day after Thanksgiving to protest the sale of furs.

DEBATED:

SHOULD WE BE ASHAMED TO WEAR FUR?

Yes. Of all the ways invented by humans to torture animals, killing them to make fur products is the most troubling. We should be ashamed to wear fur because humans do not need furs for any worthwhile purpose, and the practice of fur farming is barbaric.

Necessity. Fur clothing is a vanity product. Its major use was to keep people warm. But today, one does not need fur to keep warm. Modern industry is so easily able to provide warm clothing that does not require for its manufacture the suffering and death of animals.

There are good synthetic insulated fabrics that line coats and keep people warm. To create the fur look for those who feel a real need of it for the sake of fashion, designers have created faux furs (imitation furs). These have the appearance of real furs but are made of synthetic material. In our modern world, we can have our choice of style and live ethically, too.

Fur clothing is primarily for the wealthy. Kings and queens adorned themselves with fur in the age when monarchies ruled empires and nations. Hollywood stars wore expensive sables, mink, and ermines to project a glamorous image.

Today, monarchies have for the most part disappeared as effective political leaders, and wealthy people with a conscience refuse to wear fur. Indeed, more and more people are giving up furs. A number of designers no longer work with fur. Among them are Giorgio Armani, Bill Blass, Donna Karan, Calvin Klein, and Ralph Lauren. Nationally and internationally prominent celebrities do not wear furs. Among these celebrities are Kim

Bassinger, Elvira, Bea Arthur, and Rue McClanahan. And many fur salons have gone out of business.

The impact of ethical thinking on fur sales is striking. In 1987, domestic retail sales—sales of goods in small quantities to the consumer—for fur were $1.8 billion. Fur sales plummeted to $1 billion in 1991 and rose only to $1.2 billion in 1995. Mediamark Research, Inc., a polling company, says that 5.4 million Americans bought furs in 1993, compared to 7.6 million in 1989.

A *Los Angeles Times* poll conducted in the United States in December 1993 found that 50 percent of the people interviewed opposed the wearing of clothes made of animal fur. Only 35 percent favored wearing furs, and 15 percent expressed no opinion on the subject. Opposition was higher among women and the young than among other groups.

The popular disapproval of furs is far-reaching in American society. The lack of popularity of furs has led to some dramatic developments. In 1990, the hit game show "Wheel of Fortune" announced that it would no longer give furs away as prizes. All other game shows had already dropped fur. Mail-order houses, such as Land's End, dropped furs and many leather garments from their catalogs.

The antifur movement's success is not limited to the United States. Retail sales of fur are dropping in the United Kingdom, Germany, France, and the Netherlands.

Models from a modeling agency in New York City stage a "live supermodel billboard" to promote their agency's announcement that it is fur free.

Barbaric practices. If every woman who wore a fur coat could see how the animals are raised to produce the garment she is wearing, all women would feel ashamed to wear fur. Not only are furbearing animals confined to small cages, they are subjected to other kinds of cruel treatment, as well.

The very confinement of these animals is barbaric. Furbearers are wild animals that should not be kept in cages. Unlike dogs and cats, they have not been subjected to domestication for hundreds of years. Confinement is not natural for them. For example, wild foxes are accustomed to roaming over a dozen square miles in search of food. In captivity, they can move only a few steps. In fur farming, mink live their entire lives in small cages.

It is not only confinement that is barbaric. Farmers keep mink in artificially controlled lighting. Rather than allowing the animals to eat their food as they would in a natural setting, the farmers speed up the feeding process so that they may harvest the animal pelts quickly. Farmers even reduce the gestation period from 54 to 44 days from the gestation period in the wild. In fur farms, moreover, animals get many different diseases. These include distemper, mink virus enteritis, and pneumonia.

Finally, ranchers use horrendous methods to kill animals. Mink are killed with carbon monoxide or dioxide gas. They die in a kind of gas chamber. Foxes are killed by poisonous injection that causes the heart to stop beating. In some cases, the drugs result in animals being skinned alive. According to HSUS, ranchers often kill small animals such as mink and chinchilla by breaking their necks.

It is no wonder that the animals suffer, because few U.S. laws regulate standards of caring for ranch-raised animals. Many animals endure lingering deaths because the cost of killing them humanely is too expensive.

People should be ashamed to wear furs. When they wear furs, they show a willingness to kill animals just for the sake of vanity. Moreover, they are contributing to an industry that causes great suffering to animals.

No. An appropriate use of fur is in the manufacture of apparel. Furs make beautiful clothes. Women should wear fur if that is their choice. They have no reason to feel guilty. People who buy or wear furs should understand that fur farmers treat their animals humanely.

Necessity. Humans use animals for clothing because such use serves people's legitimate needs. Farm-bred animals are an appropriate resource for clothing, just as chickens and cattle are an appropriate resource for food.

Make no mistake about it: The real objection that animal rightists have to wearing furs is not that the furs are not needed but rather that they are an animal product. Supporters of animal rights object to any human use of animals—for clothing or anything else. They are antifur because furs are associated with wealth. But they are also against the use of wool, although sheep are not killed in order to obtain the wool. Supporters of animal rights are against killing geese for their down and other animals for leather. They feel that humans do not really need the items made from these materials.

The attempt to equate furs with wealth is only a trick used by animal rightists to oppose animal use. Animal rightists attack the fur industry because it is a popular target and not because it even involves many animals. Of the more than 6.3 billion animals used annually in the United States by humans, only 0.2 percent are used in the fur industry.

Animal rightists see in the war against furs an opportunity to use class envy as a weapon to gain popular approval for their cause. They criticize wealthy people when it serves their purpose. But we should remember that when it serves their interests, they criticize poor people, too. In this regard they identify as "slobs" poor people who hunt—even poor people who hunt for their food.

When animal rightists say that fur is not necessary and should be banned, they assume that they have a right to force their personal preferences on everybody else. One wonders what other things they might rule out as being unnecessary. Is a private automobile really necessary since we can walk, ride a bicycle, or take public transportation to move from one place to another? But we may prefer to drive a car on a trip from New York to Chicago, or from Boston to San Francisco, or between other places.

It is strange that animal rightists ignore the issue of the environment in any discussion of furs. That is strange because if we do not pay attention to environmental protection, we endanger life on our planet. If the environment were important to animal rightists, they would change their opposition to furs. Fur farming is an environmentally friendly industry. Nothing goes to waste in fur farming. Fur animal pelts are made into garments and other finished products. Fur animal carcasses are used for pet foods and farm animal feed. Other parts of the animal become components in soaps and cosmetics.

Animal rightists falsely claim that their call for people to wear faux furs is a moral one. But fake furs are made from chemicals derived from oil. Fake furs, then, are made from nonrenewable resources. Unlike fur, they are not biodegradable (capable of being broken down by natural processes). Instead, they add to the pollution problem every time a woman throws away an imitation fur product.

We can only wonder why animal rights supporters pick on furwearing to vent their fury. The moral self-righteousness of animal rightists on the fur issue is particularly aimed at women, who are the principal users of furs in clothes. Animal rightists do not harass men who wear leather shoes or jackets. Yet, both leather and fur are products of dead animals.

Animal rightists take too much credit for a decline in fur sales. But a close look at fur sales tells a different story. The reason that fur sales declined after 1987 are many and complex. Sales dropped after 1987 in part because of a recession. In this regard, sales of other high-priced goods, such as luxury cars and yachts, also declined at this time. In the period between 1989 and 1992 in which fur sales dropped by 25 percent, for example, U.S. sales of Mercedes-Benzes dropped 16 percent, Jaguars 54 percent, and Porsches 56 percent, according to an article in *Vogue*. The period between 1989 and 1992 was a period of recession. But fur sales picked up after the recession. In 1992, fur sales rose 10 percent over 1991. And they went up 10 percent in 1995 over 1994. Sales went down in 1994, but that was because of an unusually warm winter.

The fur industry was badly hit not only by a recession and warm weather but by international economic forces, as well. After 1987, furs were imported into the United States at greatly reduced prices—a factor that served to lower the dollar sales of furs.

And people approve of wearing fur, too. *USA Today* reported on January 22, 1997, the results of a poll on furs. According to the newspaper, American adults questioned about whether they agree or disagree with the idea that people should be free to choose to wear fur, 56 percent strongly agreed and 30 percent moderately agreed. Only 6 percent strongly disagreed and 5 percent moderately disagreed. (Three percent replied with the answer of "Don't know.")

Many women are not wearing furs because of fear rather than shame. Women are simply frightened of the terrorism by animal rights activists. They are afraid that if they wear a fur coat, they will be attacked by animal rights extremists. Women prefer not to be harassed. They do not want to have their clothes cut with a razor or ruined by red paint.

We should not underestimate the effect of terrorism on the fur industry. Furriers and farmers went out of business not only because of lower fur sales but also because of fears of violence and theft.

Designers, too, are frightened. Animal rightists broke into their offices and threatened to conduct media campaigns against them. That is the reason why so many designers caved in. But many of the same designers who gave up furs are being hypocritical. They continue to use shearling, which is wool that is still attached to the sheep's skin. They still use leather, suede, and other animal products in their clothes.

More and more women are taking furs out of storage and are wearing them in public. They refuse to be frightened. These women feel that they have the right to exercise their freedom.

Humane practices. The practice of people who raise animals in fur farms is humane because of government regulations and the attitudes of farmers themselves. Government regulates the care of animals on fur farms. Most states have laws dealing with the humane handling of animals. State departments of agriculture inspect fur farms. And some states, such as Minnesota, require fur farms to be licensed.

Moreover, farmers seek industry-wide certification, that is, proof that they have met certain standards. The Fur Farm Animal Welfare Coalition certifies that the pelts sold came from a certified farm, were inspected by a veterinarian, and were registered as a Merit Award Fur Farm in the United States. The merit award means that pelts were produced in strict obedience to humane farming practices as set by the Fur Farm Animal Welfare Coalition.

Furbearers raised on farms are among the best cared-for animals in the world. They receive veterinary attention and nutritious food. Farmers understand that their economic survival depends upon the health of their animals. Any farmer who abuses his or her animals—whether to raise furbearing animals to be used as clothing or to serve as food—would be committing economic suicide. As Alison Beal, the Fur Council of Canada's marketing director, explains: "If any animal isn't healthy, the pelt is the first place it shows."

Animal rightists make exaggerated or false claims about the treatment of animals on fur farms. Farmers use humane methods to kill animals quickly. The methods used to kill furbearing animals raised on farms are judged humane by the Animal Veterinary Medical Association, the appropriate veterinary group. Moreover, it is true that foxes roam for miles in the wild. But the reason that they roam is to find food. In captivity, they do not need to roam for food.

★ ☆ ★ ☆ ★

Women should not be ashamed to wear furs. In fact, they should be proud to wear furs since wearing them shows that they respect their freedom and their right not to be intimidated. They may wear furs as they wear wool clothes. They would appreciate that the animals used to produce the furs received humane treatment from fur farmers, and unlike faux fur, real fur is environmentally friendly.

Chapter 7

CONCLUSION: THE CONSEQUENCES OF ANIMAL RIGHTS

Debate: Is the Modern Animal Rights Movement Good for America?

Supporters and critics of animal rights in the United States continue to have great differences about the proper relationship between human beings and animals and how that relationship should be reflected in American society, including in science, agriculture, hunting, entertainment, and fur clothing. Supporters of each position, however, are in general agreement that the modern animal rights movement has had an immense impact on the world, and particularly on the United States. They differ in judging whether that impact has been good or bad for America.

DEBATED:

IS THE MODERN ANIMAL RIGHTS MOVEMENT GOOD FOR AMERICA?

Yes. With the emergence of the modern animal rights movement in the late 1970s and early 1980s, the American people have undergone a revolution in the way they think about and treat animals. No longer do Americans consider animals to be inanimate objects that humans can use as they please—without any limitations at all. Instead, Americans are increasingly bound to obey animal-friendly federal, state, and local laws and respond positively to popular ethical concerns about animals. People who own or use animals for private and public purposes know that they are legally and morally accountable for their treatment of animals in ways that their ancestors were not.

The modern animal rights movement is good for America in the most basic way of establishing principles of ethical concern that can guide responsible Americans for years to come. The movement has benefited science and product testing, animal agriculture, hunting, entertainment, and clothing.

Principles of ethical concern. The animal rights movement reflects the very best of ethical concerns that are in the tradition of democratic reform movements. If animal rights programs are adopted, the American way of life can only be strengthened. Moreover, the movement works through traditional democratic means to bring about peaceful change.

At its core, the animal rights movement is a progressive force in the tradition of movements to abolish slavery and to end discrimination based on race, gender, and other standards. Like speciesism today, racism and sexism were accepted principles for centuries after the colonists arrived on our shores. Gradually, however, most Americans recognized that African Americans and women should have the same rights as white males in such areas as voting, political participation, and economic opportunity.

It is not surprising, for example, that many feminist leaders supported animal rights and adopted vegetarianism. Among them were Susan B. Anthony and Elizabeth Cady Stanton. And as William Kunstler, the great civil rights attorney, noted in an August 1992 speech at the American Bar Association: "A growing revulsion against the atrocities [committed against farm animals] might well have a positive effect on reducing those practiced regularly on these shores against the aged, African Americans, poor whites, Latinos, women, lesbians and gays, social activists, Native Americans and Asians, to name but a few of our perennial pariahs."

The ideas of the animal rights movement are now becoming popularly accepted norms in American society, particularly among the young. For example, polls show that more than half of the American people believe that Americans should not wear fur clothes. And an even larger percentage of the American people disapprove of hunting. When we consider that the fur trade was an important part of the nation's wealth in the 17th century and that hunting has been a traditional American pastime since the first European settlers arrived on our shores, we can see that our nation has come a long way in changing our attitudes about ethical behavior toward animals.

What is particularly important is that the change in American thinking has come about peacefully through democratic processes. Concerned citizens have openly formed or joined organizations, such as Friends of Animals, FARM, HSUS, and PETA, that have dramatized the horrible treatment that animals endure. These citizens have conducted peaceful demonstrations, such as a march on Washington, D.C., in 1990 and the annual day-after-Thanksgiving antifur rallies in many U.S. cities. Moreover, Americans have been generous with their gifts of money and their volunteer efforts at calling attention to abuses of animals in such enterprises as scientific laboratories, farms, circuses, zoos, aquariums, and pet stores.

Supporters of animals have testified before legislative committees (government units that consider proposed laws) and appealed to executive officials at all levels of government. They have been successful in influencing legislators to pass laws that give some protection to animals. These laws include the AWA and its amendments, restrictions against hunting certain kinds of animal species, and the abolition of some practices, such as dog racing and horse-and-buggy rides. When they have not succeeded with political officials, they have turned to the courts in search of help.

In rare instances, animal rights activists engage in civil disobedience, the willful disobeying of the law and acceptance of punishment in an open, loving way. In this regard, animal rights activists have occupied the offices of federal government officials with responsibilities in laboratory animal care.

They have also occupied the offices of designers who used furs in clothing. In both cases, the purpose of the act of civil disobedience was to call attention to the abuse of animals.

It is well to recall that civil disobedience has a distinguished record in American history. Opponents of slavery, war, and racial and gender discrimination took part in such acts to call attention to their cause. The suffragists— women and men who were convinced that women should have the vote— engaged in some of the most dramatic instances of civil disobedience when in the aftermath of World War I, they chained themselves to buildings and obstructed traffic. Eventually, the Nineteenth Amendment to the Constitution, which was ratified (approved) in 1920, insured that women would have the right to vote. We can be encouraged that the movement for animal rights will produce results that will put an end to the human abuse of animals.

It is true that some animal rights activists have felt the need to act illegally, such as destroying scientific laboratories and harming property. When we understand the terrible harm that animal abusers inflict on more than 6 billion animals in the United States every year, we can understand the humanistic motivation for this kind of behavior.

However understanding nonviolent animal rights supporters may be of noble purpose, most members of the movement condemn illegal acts and hate violence. Most supporters of animal rights accept democratic principles and systems. They want to bring about peaceful change. Moreover, they fully recognize that violence and other illegal behavior work against their goals and undermine support of the animal rights movement.

Peter Singer, the father of the modern animal rights movement, is strongly opposed to the use of violence against those who use animals. He feels that if animal rights is about nonharm to living beings, then one must apply this principle to both nonhuman animals and to human animals.

Critics of the animal rights movement equate it with terrorism, but that is an unfair accusation. The animal rights movement should no more be judged in terms of its extremists than should earlier progressive movements, such as antiwar efforts. During the Vietnam War of the 1960s and 1970s, for example, some antiwar activists engaged in violence, but most did not. The acts of a few did not mean that the entire antiwar movement should be discredited.

Once we understand the peaceful, democratic nature of the animal rights movement, we can move on to judging the impact of the movement on certain parts of American society. For it is in these areas that we can see how valuable the animal rights movement has been to the American people.

Science and safety testing. Much of the strength of the modern animal rights movement stems from extreme dislike of the horrors of laboratory research and safety testing involving animals. Animal rights organizations conducted investigations of the mistreatment of animals in laboratories. Then they made public the terrible conditions that they had found. Americans were horrified when they saw the videotapes of the cruelty that scientists inflicted on animals.

Animal rights supporters continue to monitor scientific research. They are outspoken in asking whether experiments involving animals, particularly on primates and cats, are really necessary. In some cases, such as the experiments on cats conducted at the American Museum of Natural History in New York City in the 1970s, animal rights activists were able to get the support of Congress and end the research.

At the very least, animal rights supporters have been successful in getting some scientists to follow humane practices in animal care because the scientists know that someone out there is watching them. But that is not all that animal rights supporters have accomplished. One of their major achievements is that they have brought about a search for alternatives to animal research. Some examples are in vitro testing, clinical research, epidemiological studies, and computer modeling.

Animal rights activists question the necessity of using animals as test subjects for scientific research.

Animal rights groups can be proud of the effects that they have had on science education and on freedom of expression. In many areas of the country, high school students in biology classes are legally permitted to refuse to dissect animals. Students who are antivivisectionists are free to act in an ethical way without fear that the failure to kill an animal will result in a low grade.

Animal rights supporters can also be pleased with their impact on product safety testing. At first, the manufacturers of cosmetics ignored the appeals of the animal rights movement. Because of the publicity about the means the companies used to test products, particularly on rabbits, the most important cosmetic companies ended their animal tests. Instead they relied on ingredients that had been tested before or on alternatives to animal testing. Hundreds of companies now market "cruelty free" products that have not been tested on animals. Among these companies are Avon, Body Shop, Clinique, and Estée Lauder.

Although some companies continue to use animals in product safety tests, the number of animals used in such tests has fallen. The companies that do continue with these tests use more humane practices than was the case before the modern animal rights movement emerged. Some tests, such as the classic LD-50 test, are now rarely used.

The use of animals in science and in safety testing continues. But supporters of this use are on the defensive. People who believe that ethical behavior should guide scientific research can only hope that in time, all animal use in science will come to an end.

Agriculture. Animal rights supporters have been successful in making known the evils of the animal agriculture industry. They have pointed to the dreadful conditions that farmers have created in their treatment of animals. They have shown the horrors of confinement and mistreatment in the factory farms of today. They point to the battery-cage system of producing chickens and to the solitary confinement system of raising veal calves.

They have made public the damage the animal-agriculture industry causes to the environment. For example, they inform people of the role that cattle play in global warming and in the pollution of water and land resources.

Animal rights supporters can point with pride to important changes in animal agriculture. In response to animal rights criticism, in 1994, major meat-packers replaced the chaining and lifting of large conscious animals with a more humane system of upright restrainers. According to Henry Spira's Animal Rights International, "This is the first refinement of mass production methods in the meatpacking industry that takes into account the well-being of farm animals." And in 1994, McDonald's required all of its suppliers "to take all reasonable steps to assure animals raised, transported, and slaughtered for McDonald's products are treated humanely."

Significantly, the animal rights movement has pointed out the dangers of animal agriculture to the health of human beings. The nation has become aware of the relationship between diet and disease. Informed Americans now understand that because animal products contain high amounts of saturated fats, people who eat these products are more likely to get heart disease, stroke, or cancer.

Animal rightists can be grateful that the number of people who adopt vegetarian diets is increasing. More and more people demand alternatives to meat products in restaurants. People will live longer and better because of this concern with health.

Hunting. Animal rights supporters can be proud that they have changed the way that the American people think about hunting. Most Americans now oppose hunting. Hunters and trappers are on the defensive as antihunting protests get increasing national attention. Some states have limited the hunting of particular species. For example, California now limits the hunting of mountain lions. Animal rights groups have gone to court to block hunts of mountain lions, bears, and doves. And animal rightists have won support when they made known that much of the so-called conservation effort is nothing more than conserving animals that hunters want to kill.

Entertainment. The animal rights movement has publicized cruel treatment of animals in entertainment, such as horse and dog races, zoos, circuses, and rodeos. In some cases, it has been able to prevent dog racing from moving into areas where it did not exist. It has helped put an end to animal acts in which animals were badly treated. And it has drawn attention to the horrible fate that befalls animals when zoos have more animals than they can care for.

Furs. Thanks to the animal rights movement, more and more women are ashamed to wear furs. The fur industry in America has not been able to reach the high level of sales that it achieved in 1987 because furs have become identified with cruelty to animals. Many stores that used to sell furs have gone out of business, and some department stores have closed their fur departments.

Some of the famous names in the design of women's clothes no longer design in furs. The designers who have given up furs understand that women who wear faux furs, rather than real furs, are making a statement that they support the cause of animal protection.

The modern animal rights movement has been long regarded as a small group with extreme views. It has come a long way toward achieving respectability. Its cause has gained the support of so many people in

America that it is now mainstream. Many young people support certain aims of the animal rights program. Quite a number are now vegetarians. Some are against hunting. And many are opposed to the use of animals in so-called scientific research. This feeling on the part of young people suggests that the future belongs to the movement. Sentiment for animal protection may well grow to a point where most people in the United States agree with the movement. Then and only then can Americans feel proud that they follow a standard that is ethical.

NO. Few movements that claim to have high moral standards have been so wrong as animal rights. Unlike other movements that have benefited America, such as movements to achieve racial and gender equality, the animal rights movement has been harmful to the American people. It has been harmful to animals, too.

The animal rights movement is not ethical. It has caused considerable damage wherever it has had an impact. This is especially true in science and product testing, animal agriculture, hunting, entertainment, and clothing.

Principles of ethical behavior. Although claiming noble concerns about the need to protect animals, the animal rights movement is highly unethical. Moreover, a fairly high number of animal-rights supporters take part in acts of terrorism. These acts are in direct conflict with democratic processes. Many supporters of the animal rights movement sympathize with animal rights terrorism—or at least fail to speak out against it, let alone fight it.

At its core, the animal rights movement not only doesn't care about human concerns but also is actively hostile to them. Unlike the causes of civil rights for African Americans and for women, the animal rights movement is concerned not with people, but rather with animals. This is true no matter what the damage may be to human beings in the unhappy time that may come if the animal rights program becomes adopted in American laws and customs.

It is true that some supporters of the animal rights movement use democratic means of peaceful protest to achieve their goals. But many do not. Terrorism has become a central feature of the movement. Such antidemocratic illegality should not be ignored by anyone who is judging the animal rights movement.

Acting in the name of animal protection, animal rights extremists, led by ALF, have inflicted many acts of violence on the American people. Although

An anti-fur demonstrator is arrested for blocking the entrance to a fur fashion show in New York City.

lacking a united organization, its goal is to free animals and to harm those who own, use, or profit from animals—in other words, the great majority of the American people.

One study that described the extent of animal rights extremism was a report to Congress in 1993 by the Criminal Division of the Justice Department, with the assistance of the Animal and Plant Health Inspection Service of the Department of Agriculture. According to the report, between 1977 and June 30, 1993, ALF and other extremist animal rights groups were proven to have carried out 313 acts against enterprises or individuals using or marketing animals or animal-derived products. ALF took credit for about 60 percent of these incidents. The type of activity included vandalism, theft, personal threats, arson, bomb threats, fire bombs, hoax bombs, and bombing attempts.

Animal rights extremists targeted 28 different types of animal enterprises. University areas, mainly research laboratories in which animals were kept for testing, were the most frequent targets. In the order of frequency, other targets were fur shops or departments, individuals, and the food production and retail industries.

To be sure, many animal rights activists condemn the acts of terrorism. However, others are silent or give some support to these acts. PETA, for example, usually supports the motives behind the violent attacks.

Given the acts of animal rights terrorism against women, it is astonishing that supporters of animal rights see their movement as being the same as the struggle for women's rights. Animal rights extremists not only criticize women who wear furs but harass them, as well. They spray red paint on the furs or damage the furs in other ways. They do not accept women's right to freedom of choice.

There is no justification for terrorism in a democratic society. Moreover, there is no justification for civil disobedience when other means of peaceful protest are available. Comparisons with the civil rights movement for African Americans have no meaning. At the time of the major civil rights activities, African Americans in southern states were not free to exercise many rights that white Americans could. These included voting and peaceful political demonstrations. African Americans had to engage in acts of civil disobedience since they had no other legal choice. Animal rights supporters have other means of legal protest.

It is strange, too, for animal rightists to argue for freedom of choice when they try to take away freedom from people who disagree with their views. If they had their way, many supporters of animal rights would block the right of hunters to hunt, or people to take a horse-drawn carriage ride around the park, or a woman to wear fur.

The animal rights movement makes the very idea of rights seem unimportant. This does an injustice to the movement for human rights in America. At a time in which people are having real problems, animal rights organizations are collecting money to help rats and insects. Humanitarians should put their energy and money into fighting the forces that produce homelessness, joblessness, economic unfairness, and drug dependency.

Animal rights organizations make human rights seem unimportant in many ways. Most appalling are the comparisons between human use of animals and the horrors the Nazis inflicted on the Jewish people, with the murder of six million Jews. Says PETA's Ingrid Newkirk: "Six million people died in concentration camps, but six billion broiler chickens will die this year in slaughter houses."

A PETA news release echoed this view: "In time, we'll look on those who work [in animal laboratories] with the horror now reserved for the men and women who experimented on Jews in Auschwitz....That, too, the Nazis said, was 'for the greater benefit of the master race.'"

Anyone interested in human dignity would be horrified by comparing the Holocaust with a chicken dinner. Ending the consumption of chopped liver at a restaurant or the display of a giraffe at a zoo should not be a major goal. But animal rightists care nothing about human dignity.

This is not to say that people should not be concerned about the welfare of animals. They certainly should be. But they should set their priorities in order because of the terrible problems faced by people who have little chance to move out of their downtrodden condition.

Animal rights, then, is a movement that is unethical and is at war with the democratic process. To get a more accurate understanding of the evils of animal rights, we need to look at the terrible consequences that the animal rights movement has produced in certain parts of American society.

Science and safety testing. Animals have been used in medical research to find cures for some of the deadliest of diseases, including heart disease, diphtheria, diabetes, and yellow fever. The FDA regards animal tests as so vital that it requires all medicines to be tested on animals. The FDA does not accept nonanimal tests as good enough.

Animals are now being used in the search to find a cure for AIDS. But Ingrid Newkirk reflects the view of the animal rights movement when she says that even if animal research would find a cure for AIDS, "we'd be against it."

Rarely do animal rights leaders make such statements because they reveal that animal rightists would rather allow hundreds of thousands of people die from a curable disease than take the life of a rat, chimpanzee, or other animal. Usually, animal rightists argue that alternatives to animal research are as good as—if not better than—animal research. In holding this view, however, they go against the overwhelming opinion of medicine, as surveys of the attitudes of doctors show.

The harsh reality of the consequences of the animal rights movement is that people will die because of what the animal rights movement has accomplished. Animals will die, too, since animal research benefits them. Animal rights activists hinder the finding of cures for serious illnesses in many ways, but the most important is by forcing increases in the cost of medical research. The costs of animals in research have risen because of increased government regulations, in such matters as cage size and requiring research institutions to care for the "psychological well-being" of primates. According to the

American Medical Association, in 1990 the costs of obeying new government rules for the care of research animals made up 20 percent of the federal medical research budget. That 20 percent represented $1.5 billion.

Some states have further increased costs by adding unnecessary restrictions. For example, some state pound laws forbid pounds from selling animals to research organizations. In these states, not only are the animals going to be killed anyway if no one claims them, but the researchers must go elsewhere to purchase animals at high cost.

Medical research is slowed down not only by government rules but by terrorism, as well. Because of the many acts of vandalism and destruction of laboratory research, universities and other institutions engaged in animal research have had to pay large amounts of money for increased security. According to a survey by the Association of American Medical Colleges in 1991, the activities of animal activists cost America's medical schools about $10 million in the period between 1986 and 1991. Medical schools were spending over $15 million a year for security, public education, and other efforts to defend research. Money spent on obeying government rules and increased security often comes out of the research budget, which otherwise would have been spent on direct research on deadly diseases.

Still, the major goal of animal rights in medicine—to end all animal research—has not been achieved. Nor is it likely to be. Animal rights activists may protest outside of a hospital in such matters as the transplanting of a baboon's heart to a human being in order to save the life of a human, but most people would approve of this procedure if it gave the patient a chance to live.

The animal rights movement has taken a terrible toll on the scientific education of the nation's youth by contributing to ignorance about science. Dissection is a necessary practice in high school classes in biology. Most teachers of biology realize the importance of dissection to a student's understanding of body components.

Allowing students to choose not to take part in dissection because of moral reasons may be dangerous for education in all kinds of fields. Just think what could happen if students should decide for themselves about what is ethical in a school curriculum. Should students whose religious beliefs accept all the words of the Bible as exact historical truth be allowed to refuse to study evolution just because evolution may be against their religious teaching? Should Jewish students not be required to listen to the works of Richard Wagner in a music course because Wagner was an anti-Semite? Without damaging the basis of education itself, it simply is not possible to arrange a class in which some student would reject to a legitimate educational requirement.

In the matter of product safety testing, animal rights supporters have caused some serious cutbacks in the use of animals for safety tests. But, as indicated in Chapter 2, many of their claims are false. It is true that major cosmetic companies have stopped using animal research in developing new products. However, many of them get around this requirement by using ingredients that have already been tested on animals, or which are tested by other companies.

Many companies seek to use alternatives to animal research to assure safety for their products. In fact, the cosmetics industry has been a principal supporter of research relying on alternatives to animals. General Motors no longer uses animals in trauma (physical injury) testing because its testing project has been completed. But it continues to use animals in toxicity (poison) testing.

Many companies continue to use animals in product safety testing because they know that it is the only way to assure safety in many kinds of cases. They recognize that legally they are responsible for producing items that are safe for fear that they may be subjected to costly lawsuits by the people who have been injured by the product.

Scientists and companies that produce items, such as soaps and shampoos, will continue to use animals in testing, so long as such use is necessary to achieve their goals. The American people will approve whatever it takes to assure that they get the greatest medical benefits and the greatest safety from the products that they use.

Agriculture. Animal agriculture remains a thriving industry in spite of the effects of the animal rights movement. Americans have reduced the amount of red meat that they eat. But the great majority of them continue to eat red meat. Where they have stopped eating red meat, they have turned to poultry and fish—two products that are not acceptable food to animal rightists.

It is true that an increasing number of people are vegetarians. But even many people who call themselves vegetarians continue to eat animal products such as milk and eggs.

People eat animal products because they are nutritious and healthy. Dietitians and medical experts recognize that animal products, when taken as part of an overall approved diet, are healthy foods.

The good health movement, which has called attention to excessive saturated fats in a diet, arose independently of the animal rights movement.

Attention to good health requires that a person take care not to eat too many animal products, rather than to give up all animal products.

Hunting. The antihunting supporters have not put an end to hunting and trapping. In spite of efforts by animal rightists supporters to spoil hunting by scaring away animals, hunters continue to hunt. Hunters also contribute money to help conservation programs.

The antihunt movement has hurt the environment, too. In Louisiana, the decline in the market for nutria (a large beaverlike rodent) has resulted in an overpopulation of this furbearing animal. Nutria are destroying the marshlands and are causing a population decline in many endangered shorebirds and sea turtles. The overpopulation of some species of animals, brought on by limitations on the methods that may be used in culling animal populations, has resulted in a destruction of property and a terrible death for the animals because of the resulting lack of food and shelter.

Many states have passed antihunter harassment laws because of the danger that animal rights activists pose to the safety of hunters. The courts have upheld the constitutionality of these laws.

Entertainment. Animal rights supporters have received some publicity points when animals are injured or killed in zoos, aquariums, circuses, and rodeos. However, for the most part, animals continue to do well in these environments. Zoos have become modernized and contribute to the continuing existence of species, as for example the California condor. Circuses continue to delight young and old people alike. And rodeos are thriving.

Nutria overpopulation has caused significant damage to the environment.

Furs. Fur sales in the United States went down for a few years after 1987, but rose after 1990. The decline in sales for the industry was caused by many factors having nothing to do with the animal rights protests—factors, such as tough competition and an oversupply of pelts.

Although some celebrities have tried to shame people for wearing furs, there are signs that women are tired of the harassment to which they have been subjected. In the inauguration parties in honor of the election of Bill Clinton as President of the United States in 1993, a number of guests happily wore furs. And some well-known celebrities have posed for advertisements of fur garments. Although the 1994 year saw a decline in the sale of fur coats, this decline was caused mostly by an unusually warm winter. Fur sales increased in 1995 and 1996.

The animal rights movement has had an impact on American society, but that impact has been harmful to the values that the nation cherishes. We can only hope that support for the movement has reached its peak.

One of the unexpected results of the movement was to produce a response by the groups that were the victims or targets of the animal rights movement. At first, the targets did not recognize the threat that they faced. In some cases, they hoped that the animal rights movement would go away. They soon realized that they had to unite and take action.

These groups were eager to tell their side of the story. Medical researchers emphasized the importance of their work to the health of both people and animals. Cosmetic and pharmaceutical companies showed the necessity of animal testing to assure that people do not get killed or hurt. They also provided money for research on alternatives to animal research. They made clear that if these alternatives worked, they would use them. (Besides, they knew that the alternatives might be less costly than animal research. So the companies would have an economic incentive to use them.)

Groups dealing with animals told their story. Farmers explained their humane practices in caring for animals. Hunters and trappers stressed their contributions to the environment and to conservation of resources. Zoos and aquariums described their contributions to the preservation of animal species. And furriers emphasized the humane means that hunters and fur farmers use in caring for their furbearing animals.

Many organizations were formed to make the case for the human use of animals. In 1979, the National Association for Biomedical Research (NABR) and the Foundation for Biomedical Research were founded to fight animal rights and to defend animal research for scientific purposes. Incurably Ill for Animal Research and the Coalition for Animals and Animal Research were formed to defend the use of animals in medical testing. New organizations were formed, such as Putting People First, whose sole purpose was to fight the animal rights movement. Cosmetic companies, farm groups, hunters and trappers, zoos, and rodeos designed public relations programs to get their side of the story heard.

Leading figures in the health and science communities became spokespersons for the cause of animal research. Among them were Louis H. Sullivan, the secretary of the Department of Health and Human Services in the administration of President George Bush, and C. Everett Koop, Surgeon General in the administration of Ronald Reagan. Frederick Goodwin of the Alcohol, Drug Abuse and Mental Health Administration helped to create a new office for animal research in his office at the NIH.

Congress, too, began to listen. In 1990, for example, members of the House of Representatives formed the Animal Welfare Caucus under the leadership of then Congressman Vin Weber (Republican of Minnesota).

Legislative feeling against the acts of terrorism became so strong that Congress passed major laws to deal with it. In August 1992, President Bush signed into law the Animal Enterprise Protection Act, making it a federal offense, punishable by fine and/or imprisonment of up to one year, to cause physical disruption to the functioning of an animal enterprise resulting in economic damage exceeding $10,000. The act also imposes sentences of up to ten years or life imprisonment, respectively, on persons causing the serious bodily injury or death of another person during the course of such an offense. The law covered animal agriculture, research facilities, zoos, and other enterprises using animals.

The animal rights movement has taken credit for reforms in the treatment of animals for which it has played no role or at best a limited role. Humane groups, motivated by animal welfare, deserve credit for changes in the way humans treat animals. Supporters of animal welfare in the scientific, agricultural, entertainment, and fur industry, and in other sectors of American society, who care about animals but who do not believe that they should have rights equal to human rights, deserve the credit for improving the conditions of animals.

ABBREVIATIONS

ADC	Animal Damage Control
AIDS	Aquired Immunodeficiency Syndrome
ALF	Animal Liberation Front
AMA	American Medical Association
ASPCA	American Society for the Prevention of Cruelty to Animals
AWA	Animal Welfare Act
AZA	American Zoo and Aquarium Association
BST	Bovine somatotropin
FBI	Federal Bureau of Investigation
FDA	Food and Drug Administration
HSUS	The Humane Society of the United States
NABR	National Association for Biomedical Research
NIH	National Institutes of Health
OTA	Office of Technology Assessment
PETA	People for the Ethical Treatment of Animals
PHS	Public Health Service
SSP	Species Survival Program
USDA	U.S. Department of Agriculture

GLOSSARY

agribusiness The huge industry of agriculture.

amphibians Cold-blooded animals such as frogs and toads.

anatomy The science of the body structure of plants and animals.

anemia A condition in which blood lacks enough red blood cells.

anesthetized Given anesthesia, which produces a loss of sensation.

animal agriculture The business of raising and selling animals mostly for food.

animal conservation The preservation of a species so that it has sufficient resources to survive.

animal protection groups Groups with a commitment to animal care, whether animal rights or animal welfare.

animal rights The philosophy that animals should have the same rights, or equivalent consideration, as humans.

animal welfare The view that humans possess a right to own or use animals but must do so in a humane way.

anthropomorphism An attempt to see animals as having thoughts and feelings.

battery cages A series of connected cages.

biodegradable Capable of being broken down by natural processes.

bioengineering The use of engineering in biology.

biomedicine Medicine as it relates to all biological systems.

branding The burning of a symbol into the flesh of an animal.

cadavers Dead human beings.

canned hunt Any hunt in a human-constructed enclosure where the animal has no chance of escape.

carnivores Flesh-eating mammals.

cholesterol A substance that exists in the fat, tissue, and blood in all animals.

chromosomes The structures in cells that carry genes.

computer modeling The use of the computer to duplicate the features of humans or animals without having to experiment with humans or animals.

cull Reduce an animal's population.

debeak To burn the tip of a chicken's beak with a hot iron.

dehorning The removal of cattle's horns.

desertification The process by which an area becomes a desert.

dietitians Specialists in food quality and diet.

due process A legal principle that assures constitutional guarantees against the arbitrary taking of life, liberty, or property.

ecosystem A system of relationships among plants, animals, and the environment.

enzymes The substances that speed up the chemical reactions of living cells.

epidemiological studies Investigations of naturally occurring disease patterns within populations.

evolution The belief that existing organisms descended from a common ancestor.

faux furs Imitation furs.

fetus The unborn young.

free-range system A system in which chickens are allowed to move around over a large area rather than be confined to a small area.

genetic engineers Scientists who work to alter genetic material.

gestation Pregnancy.

government grants Money to pay for research.

greenhouse effect This effect occurs when gases, such as methane, carbon dioxide, nitrogen oxides, and ozone, rise into the atmosphere, thus slowing the rate at which heat escapes from the Earth.

habitat The natural environment of a life form that allows it to live and grow.

hemophilia A disease marked by excessive bleeding.

herbivores Plant-eating mammals.

immune system A network of cells that protects the body from harmful substances.

inbreeding The mating of closely related animals.

incubation The time needed to hatch or develop.

in vitro research A type of research that does not use live animals.

lactose Milk sugar.

legislative committees Government units that consider proposed laws.

legumes Plant products, such as beans, peas, lentils, peanuts, and soybeans.

natural laws Laws that are fundamental to human nature.

omnivores Mammals that eat both animal flesh and plant food.

osteoporosis A disease causing the loss of bone-tissue mass.

pediatrics The branch of medicine dealing with the care of children and the treatment of childhood diseases.

poachers Illegal hunters.

predators Animals that live by killing other animals for food.

rabies An infectious disease of warm-blooded animals that attacks the central nervous system.

racism The philosophy that one race is superior to another.

salmonella Bacteria that can poison people.

saturated fat A type of animal or vegetable fat that increases the cholesterol level in humans.

sexism A philosophy that asserts that one gender is superior to another.

sow An adult female hog.

speciesism A philosophy asserting the exclusive interests of the human species over nonhuman species.

suffragists Women and men who campaigned for women to have the vote.

teratology The science that addresses the causes of birth defects.

toxic Poisonous.

utilitarianism A philosophy that holds that a moral act should be judged on the basis of its consequences.

vegans People who do not eat any animal products.

vegetarianism The practice or belief in living on a diet consisting mostly of vegetable products, fruits, grains, and seeds.

vertebrates Animals having a backbone or spinal column.

vivisection The dissecting or experimenting with live animals for medical research.

xenography The transplantation of healthy body parts of animals to humans with comparable, but diseased, body parts, such as the heart and the liver.

BIBLIOGRAPHY

Chapter 1: The World of Animal Rights

Fox, Michael W. *Inhumane Society: The American Way of Exploiting Animals.* New York: St. Martin's Press, 1990.

Fraser, Laura, et al. *The Animal Rights Handbook: Everyday Ways to Save Animal Lives.* Los Angeles, CA: Living Planet Press, 1990.

Howard, Walter E. *Animal Rights Vs. Nature.* Davis, CA: Walter E. Howard, 1990.

Jasper, James M., and Dorothy Nelkin. *The Animal Rights Crusade: The Growth of a Moral Protest.* New York: Free Press, 1992.

McCabe, Katie. "Beyond Cruelty." *Washingtonian* 25 (Feb. 1990): 72, 77, 185–187, 189–195.

Oliver, Charles. "Liberation Zoology." *Reason* 22 (June 1990): 22–27.

Regan, Tom. *The Case for Animal Rights.* Berkeley: University of California Press, 1983.

Rollin, Bernard E. *Animal Rights and Human Morality*, rev. ed. Buffalo, NY: Prometheus Books, 1992.

Ryder, Richard D. *Animal Revolution: Changing Attitudes Toward Speciesism.* London: Basil Blackwell, 1989.

Salt, Henry S. *Animals' Rights Considered in Relation to Social Progress.* Clarks Summit, PA: Society for Animal Rights, 1980. (Originally published in 1892.)

Sherry, Clifford J. *Animal Rights: A Reference Handbook.* Santa Barbara, CA: ABC-CLIO, 1994.

Singer, Peter. *Animal Liberation: A New Ethic for Our Treatment of Animals*, 2nd ed. New York: New York Review of Books, 1990. (First edition published in 1975.)

————, ed. *In Defense of Animals.* New York: Basil Blackwell, 1985.

Strand, Rod and Patti. *The Hijacking of the Humane Movement.* Wilsonville, OR: Doral Publishing, 1993.

Turner, James. *Reckoning with the Beast: Animals, Pain and Humanity in the Victorian Mind.* Baltimore, MD: Johns Hopkins University Press, 1980.

Chapter 2: Animals in Science

Baird, Robert M., and Stuart E. Rosenbaum, eds. *Animal Experimentation: The Moral Issues.* Buffalo, NY: Prometheus Books, 1991.

Balcombe, Jonathan. "Education by Extermination." *Animals' Agenda* 14 (Sept./Oct. 1994), pp. 22–25.

Blum, Deborah. *The Monkey Wars.* New York: Oxford University Press, 1994.

Burch, R.L., and W.M.S. Russell. *The Principles of Humane Experimental Technique.* London: Methuen, 1959.

Cavalieri, Paola, and Peter Singer, eds. *The Great Ape Project: Equality Beyond Humanity.* New York: St. Martin's Press, 1994.

Cohen, Carl. "The Case for the Use of Animals in Biomedical Research." *New England Journal of Medicine* 315 (Oct. 2, 1986): 865–870.

Fox, Michael A. *The Case for Animal Experimentation: An Evolutionary and Ethical Perspective.* Berkeley: University of California Press, 1986.

Francione, Gary L., and Anna E. Charlton. *Vivisection and Dissection in the Classroom: A Guide to Conscientious Objection.* Jenkintown, PA: American Anti-Vivisection Society, 1992.

Fraser, Caroline. "The Raid at Silver Spring." *New Yorker* 69 (Apr. 19, 1993), 66–74, 76–84.

Goldberg, Alan M., and John M. Frazier. "Alternatives to Animals in Toxicity Testing." *Scientific American* 261 (Aug. 1989), 24–30.

Guillermo, Kathy S. *Monkey Business: The Disturbing Case That Launched the Animal Rights Movement.* Washington, D.C.: National Press Books, 1993.

Hubbell, John G. "The 'Animal Rights' War on Medicine." *Reader's Digest,* 136 (June 1990), 70–76.

Morrison, Adrian R. "Biomedical Research and the Animal Rights Movement: A Contrast in Values." *The American Biology Teacher* 55 (Apr. 1993): 204–208.

Nicoll, Charles S., and Sharon M. Russell. "Animal Rights, Animal Research, and Human Obligations." *Molecular and Cellular Neurosciences* 3 (1992): 271–277.

Orlans, F. Barbara. *In the Name of Science: Issues in Responsible Animal Experimentation.* New York: Oxford University Press, 1993.

Rollin, Bernard E. *The Unheeded Cry: Animal Consciousness, Animal Pain and Science.* New York: Oxford University Press, 1989.

Rowan, Andrew N., Franklin M. Rowe, with Joan C. Weer. *The Animal Research Controversy: Protest, Process & Public Policy: An Analysis of Strategic Issues.* North Grafton, MA: Center for Animals & Public Policy, Tufts University School of Veterinary Medicine, 1995.

Todd, Betsy. "Animal Research and Aids." *NAVS* [New England Antivivisection Society] *Bulletin,* Dec. 1994, 18–19.

White, Robert J. "The Facts About Animal Research." *Reader's Digest,* 132 (Mar. 1988), 127–132.

Chapter 3: Animal Agriculture

Blakely, James, and David H. Bade. *The Science of Animal Husbandry,* 6th ed. Englewood Cliffs, NJ: Prentice Hall Career and Technology, 1994.

Burros, Marian. "Cow's Milk and Children: A New No-No?" *New York Times,* Sept. 30, 1992, pp. C1, C6.

Cheeke, Peter R. *Impacts of Livestock Production on Society, Diet/Health and the Environment.* Danville, IL: Interstate Publishers, 1993.

Coats, C. David. *Old MacDonald's Factory Farm: The Myth of the Traditional Farm and the Shocking Truth About Animal Suffering in Today's Agribusiness.* New York: Continuum, 1989.

Durning, Alan B., and Holly B. Brough. "Taking Stock: Animal Farming and the Environment." *Worldwatch Paper* No. 103. Washington, D.C.: Worldwatch Institute, July 1991.

Fox, Michael W. *Agricide: The Hidden Crisis That Affects Us All*, 2nd ed. Malabar, FL: Krieger Pub. Co., 1995.

Herren, Ray V. *The Science of Animal Agriculture*. Albany, NY: Delmar Publishers, 1994.

Inglis, Les. *Diet for a Gentle World: Eating with Conscience*. Garden City Park, NY: Avery Publishing Group, 1993.

Johnson, Andrew. *Factory Farming*. Oxford, Eng.: Basil Blackwell, 1991.

Mason, Jim, and Peter Singer. *Animal Factories*, rev. ed. New York: Harmony Books, 1990.

Rifkin, Jeremy. *Beyond Beef: The Rise and Fall of the Cattle Culture*. New York: Dutton, 1992.

Robbins, John. *Diet for a New America*. Walpole, NH: Stillpoint, 1987.

Taylor, Robert E. *Beef Production and Management Decisions*, 2nd ed. New York: Macmillan, 1994.

Chapter 4: Hunting Animals

Conniff, Richard. "Fuzzy-Wuzzy Thinking About Animal Rights." *Audubon* 92 (Nov. 1990): 120–133.

Dizard, Jan E. *Going Wild: Hunting, Animal Rights, and the Contested Meaning of Nature*. Amherst: University of Massachusetts Press, 1994.

Gassett, José Ortega y. *Meditations on Hunting*, trans. Howard B. Westcott. New York: Charles Scribner's Sons, 1972.

Howard, Walter E. "Animal Rights Vs. Hunters." *Outdoor Life* (April 1991): 111.

Hummel, Richard. *Hunting and Fishing for Sport: Commerce, Controversy, Popular Culture*. Bowling Green, OH: Bowling Green State University Popular Press, 1994.

Laylock, George. *The Hunters and the Hunted*. New York: Meredith Press, 1990.

Lynge, Finn. *Arctic Wars, Animal Rights, Endangered Species*. Hanover, NH: Dartmouth College (published by University Press of New England), 1992.

McIntyre, Thomas. *The Way of the Hunter: The Art and Spirit of Modern Hunting*. New York: E.P. Dutton, 1988.

Pacelle, Wayne. "Wildlife Mismanagement." *Animals' Agenda* 11 (Sept. 1991), 12–15, 17–18.

Posewitz, Jim. *Beyond Fair Chase: The Ethic and Tradition of Hunting*. Helena, MT: Falcon Press, 1994.

Povilitis, Dr. Tony. "Living with Deer." *HSUS News* 34 (Fall 1989): 24–27.

Satchell, Michael. "The American Hunter Under Fire." *U.S. News & World Report* 108, (Feb. 5, 1990): 30–31, 33–36.

Swan, James A. *In Defense of Hunting*. San Francisco, CA: Harper SanFrancisco, 1995.

Chapter 5: Animals in Entertainment

Bostock, Stephen St. C. *Zoos and Animal Rights: The Ethics of Keeping Animals*. New York: Routledge, 1993.

Carlson, Peter. "Animal House: Backstage at the National Zoo." *Washington Post Magazine*, June 17, 1990: 14–21, 31–34.

Fox, Michael W. "The Trouble with Zoos." *Animals' Agenda* 6 (1986): 8–12.

Grandy, John W. "Captive Breeding in Zoos: Destructive Programs in Need of Change." *HSUS News* 34 (Summer 1989): 8–11.

_____. "Zoos: A Critical Reevaluation." *HSUS News* 37 (Summer 1992): 12–14.

Koebner, Linda. *The Zoo Book: The Evolution of Wildlife Conservation Centers.* New York: T. Doherty, 1994.

Luoma, Jon R. *A Crowded Ark: The Role of Zoos in Wildlife Conservation.* Boston, MA: Houghton Mifflin, 1987.

Maier, Franz, and Jake Page. *Zoo: The Modern Ark.* New York: Facts on File, 1990.

Maple, Terry L., and Erika F. Archibald. *Zoo Man: Inside the Revolution.* Atlanta, GA: Longstreet Press, 1993.

Myers, Norman. *The Sinking Ark: A New Look at the Problem of Disappearing Species.* New York: Pergamon, 1979.

Norton, Bryan G., et al., eds. *Zoos, Animal Welfare, and Wildlife Conservation.* Washington, D.C.: Smithsonian Institution Press, 1995.

Tarpy, Cliff. "New Zoos: Taking Down the Bars." *National Geographic* 184 (July 1993): 2–37.

Wiese, Robert J., and Michael Hutchins. *Species Survival Plans: Strategies for Wildlife Conservation.* Wheeling, WV: American Association of Zoological Parks and Aquariums, 1994.

Chapter 6: Furry Animals

Balzar, John. "Creatures Great and—Equal?" *Los Angeles Times* (December 25, 1993): A1, A30.

Clifton, Merritt. "Fur Farms: Where the Sun Doesn't Shine." *Animals' Agenda* 11 (November 1991): 12–15.

Ferguson, Sarah. "Strike a Pose." *New York* 27 (November 7, 1994): 60–66.

Gabriel, Trip. "Such a Nice Zealot." *New York Times* (May 1, 1994): Sec. 9, 1, 8.

Gandee, Charles. "PETAphilia." *Vogue* 184 (July 1994): 28, 30.

Linden, Patricia. "The Other Side of the Anti-Fur Furor." *Ultra* 9 (October 1989): 70–71, 96, 118–119.

Marquardt, Kathleen. "From the Trenches." *Fur Age Weekly* (December 5, 1994): 18.

"Protest Passé." *Fur Age Weekly* (December 5, 1994): 2–3.

Span, Paula. "The Year the Fur Flew." *Washington Post* (April 1, 1994): D1, D2.

Szabo, Julia. "Coming in from the Cold: A Fur Lover's Backlash." *New York Times,* (December 11, 1994): 67, 71.

Chapter 7: Conclusion: The Consequences of Animal Rights

Adams, Carol J. *Neither Man Nor Beast: Feminism and the Defense of Animals.* New York: Continuum, 1994.

The Animal Rights Handbook: Everyday Ways to Save Animal Lives. Los Angeles, CA: Living Planet Press, 1990.

Francione, Gary. "Animal Rights and Animal Welfare: Five Frequently Asked Questions." *Animals' Agenda* 14 (May/June 1994): 28–29.

Hardy, David T. "America's New Extremists: What You Need to Know About the Animal Rights Movement." Washington, D.C.: Washington Legal Foundation, 1990.

Hubbell, John G. "The 'Animal Rights' War on Medicine." *Readers Digest* 136 (June 1990): 70–76.

Johnson, Rebecca. "Animal Rights, Animal Wrongs." *Mademoiselle* 101 (January 1995): 112–117.

Kunstler, William M. "From Civil Rights to Animal Rights: A Revolution." *Animals' Agenda* 13 (March/April 1993): 25–27, 43.

Leepson, Marc. "Animal Rights." *CQ Researcher* 1 (May 24, 1991): 301–324.

Lutherer, Lorenz, and Margaret Sheffield Simon. *Targeted: The Anatomy of an Animal Rights Attack.* Norman: University of Oklahoma Press, 1992.

Marquardt, Kathleen, Herbert M. Levine, and Mark LaRochelle. *AnimalScam: The Beastly Abuse of Human Rights.* Washington, D.C.: Regnery Gateway, 1993.

Newkirk, Ingrid. *Free the Animals: The Untold Story of the U.S. Animal Liberation Front and Its Founder "Valerie."* Chicago, IL: Noble Press, 1992.

_____. *Save the Animals: 101 Easy Things You Can Do.* New York: Warner Books, 1990.

Screaming Wolf (pseud.). *A Declaration of War: Killing People to Save Animals and the Environment.* Grass Valley, CA: Patrick Henry Press, 1991.

Spiegel, Marjorie. *The Dreaded Comparison: Human and Animal Slavery.* New York: Mirror Books, 1988.

FURTHER READING

Bloyd, Sunni. *Animal Rights.* San Diego, CA: Lucent, 1990

Catalano, Julie. *Animal Welfare.* Broomall, PA: Chelsea House, 1994

Cohen, Daniel. *Animal Rights: A Handbook for Young Adults.* Brookfield, CT: Millbrook, 1993

Day, Nancy. *Animal Experimentation: Cruelty or Science?* Springfield, NJ: Enslow, 1994

Field, Shelly. *Careers As an Animal Rights Activist.* Baltimore, MD: Rosen, 1993

Harnacks, Andrew, ed. *Animal Rights: Opposing Viewpoints.* San Diego, CA: Greenhaven, 1996

McCoy, J. J. *Animals in Research: Issues and Conflicts.* Danbury, CT: Franklin Watts, 1993

Owen, Marna. *Animal Rights: Yes or No.* Minneapolis, MN: Lerner, 1994

INDEX

Note: Entries in bold type
indicate photographs.

abuse, definition of, 11
agribusiness
    See animal agriculture
AIDS research, 31, 39–40, 111
Alcohol, Drug Abuse and Mental Health
        Administration, 116
American Anti-Vivisection Society, 13
American Humane Association, 18
American Medical Association (AMA)
    Committee for the Protection of Animal
        Research, 19
American Society for the Prevention of
        Cruelty to Animals (ASPCA), 13
American Zoo and Aquarium Association
        (AZA), 79–80
    Code of Professional Ethics, 87
    Species Survival Program (SSP), 88
animal, definition of, 9
animal agriculture, 44–59
    arguments against
        animals are abused, 47–49, 106
        environment is damaged by, 51–53
        food products are unhealthy, 49–51,
            106–107
    arguments for
        animals are treated humanely, 53–55
        environment is not damaged by,
            57–59
        food products are healthy, 55–57, 116
Animal Damage Control (ADC), 61
Animal Enterprise Protection Act, 116
Animal Liberation (Singer), 14
Animal Liberation Front (ALF), 18–19, 109
animal protection groups, 13–14, 18–19
animal research, 20–43
    arguments against
        alternatives are available, 30–31, 105
        animals are abused, 25–28, 105
        is unethical, 24–25
        value is questionable, 28–33
    arguments for
        alternatives are unreliable, 41–42

animals are treated humanely, 35–37
is ethical, 33–34
results are valuable, 38–41
See also medical research
animal rights movement
    compared to antiwar movement, 104
    compared to civil rights movement,
        24–25
    historical perspective of, 12–18
    negative effects of
        environment is damaged by, 114
        product safety testing is hampered,
            113
        scientific research is hampered,
            111–113
        terrorist acts by supporters, 108–111
    philosophy of supporters, 6–12
    positive effects of
        alternative research methods used, 106
        animal agriculture modified, 106–107
        animal entertainment industry
            modified, 107
        ethical principles applied, 102–104
        hunting practices modified, 107
animals in entertainment, 75–90
    arguments against
        animals are abused, 79–81
        education is not improved, 83–84
        endangered species are not preserved,
            81–83
    arguments for
        animals are treated humanely, 85–87
        education is improved, 89–90
        endangered species are preserved,
            87–89
*Animals' Rights Considered in Relation to
        Human Progress* (Salt), 14
animal testing, cost of, 38
Animal Veterinary Medical Association, 99
animal welfare
    definition of, 10
    philosophy of supporters, 10–11
Animal Welfare Act (AWA), 14, 27, 36, 103
Animal Welfare Caucus, 116

Animal Welfare Institute, 14
Anthony, Susan B., 103
anthropomorphism, definition of, 55
antifur demonstrations, 6, **93**
aquariums, 76–78, 79–81, 84–90
   See also animals as entertainment
Armani, Giorgio, 94
Arthur, Bea, 96
Assateague Island National Seashore,
   Virginia, 68
Association of American Medical Colleges,
   112
Audubon, John James, 72
Avon, 16, 106

Band of Mercy, 19
Bassinger, Kim, 95
battery-cage system, 49, **54**
Beal, Alison, 99
Bentham, Jeremy, 12
Bergen, Candice, 92
Bergh, Henry, **13**
bioengineering, definition of, 49
biomedicine, definition of, 35
birth-control vaccines, 68, 74
birth defects, 29
bison population, **72**
Blass, Bill, 94
bovine somatotropin (BST), 49, 57
Bush, George, 60, 116
Buxton, Thomas Fowell (Sir), 13
Byers, F. M., 58

California condor, **87**–88, 89
Carter, Jimmy, 60
Case for Animal Rights, The (Regan), 15
cattle growth hormone, 49, 57
Center for Alternatives to Animal Testing
   (CAAT), 16
cholesterol, definition of, 50
circuses, 75
civil disobedience, 104, 110
civil rights compared to animal rights, 25,
   110
clinical research, 30, 40
Clinique, 106
Clinton, Bill, 60
Coalition for Animals and Animal
   Research, 116
computer modeling, 30–31, 41
conservation, 66–67, 71–73

contamination of animal products, 50
cosmetics industry, 16, 30, 42, 106
Cosmetic, Toiletry, and Fragrance
   Association, 16
Council for Agricultural Science and
   Technology, 52
Cousteau, Jacques, 84
Crawford, Cindy, 92
Cruelty to Animals Act, 13

Darwin, Charles, 12
deer, overpopulation of, 69, 70– **71, 74**
DeRose, Chris, 41
Descartes, René, 12
Dickson, Andrew, 81
dissection, 13, 23, 43
   is necessary to education, 112
   is unnecessary, 32–33
   See also vivisection
dog racing, 78
Draize, John H., 26
Draize test, 26, 30, 37, 41
Durning, Alan B., 52

Earthsave, 52
E. coli infection, 50
ecosystem, definition of, 57
educational use of animals, 23, 27, 32, 43
Elvira, 95
endangered species, 65, 73, 82–83, 87–88
environmental damage, 51–52
epidemiological studies, 31, 41
Estée Lauder, 16, 106
ethics
   animal rights argument, 24–25, 102–104
   animal welfare argument, 33–34,
      108–111
evolution, definition of, 12
experimental use of animals, 15–16, 18
   See also animal research
extremist groups, 110–111
Eytex system, 30

farm animals, treatment of, 47–49, 53–55
farming
   See animal agriculture
faux furs, 94, 98, 100
Food and Drug Administration (FDA), 26
food poisoning, 50
Foundation for Biomedical Research,
   19, 115

Francis of Assisi, St., 12
Friends of Animals, 14, 103
Fund for Animals, 66
fur clothing industry
    arguments against
        alternative products are available,
            94–95
        animals are abused, 95–96
    arguments for
        animals are treated humanely, 99–100
        serves a legitimate need, 96–97
Fur Council of Canada, 99
Fur Farm Animal Welfare Coalition, 92–93,
    99
fur sales, decline of, 95, 98–99

Goodwin, Frederick, 116
Grandy, John, 81–82
greenhouse effect, 52, 59
Grinnell, George, 72

Hegins, Pennsylvania, 65, 70
Holocaust, 110
horse racing, 76
Hsing-Hsing (panda), **82**
Humane Slaughter Act, 14
Humane Society of the United States
    (HSUS), 14, 81–82, 103
Hunter Education Association, 65
hunting, 60–74
    accidents, 65, 71
    arguments against
        alternatives are available, 67–68
        animals are abused, 63–65
        environment is damaged by, 65–66
    arguments for
        alternatives are not practical, 73–74
        animals are treated humanely, 69–71
        environment benefits from, 71–73
    historical reasons for, 60, 103
    ranches, 81

Iditarod, 76
Incurably Ill for Animal Research, 116
Institute for Behavioral Research, 16
insulin, 21, **35**, 40
*Introduction to the Principles of Morals and
    Legislation* (Bentham), 12
in vitro testing, 30, 41

Karan, Donna, 94
Keillor, Garrison, 44
Kelsey, Frances, 39
Kentucky Derby, 76
Klein, Calvin, 94
Kleinman, Robert, 56
Koop, C. Everett, 39, 116
Kunstler, William, 103

Laboratory Animal Welfare Act, 14
Lagerfeld, Kurt, 92
Langley, Gill, 30
Last Chance for Animals, 41
Lauren, Ralph, 94
laws
    animal protection, 13–14, 27, 36–37, 61,
        103
LD-50 test, 26, 37, 41, 106
lead poisoning, 65, 72
Lee, Ronnie, 19
Leopold, Aldo, 72
Ling-Ling (panda), **82**
Los Angeles Zoo, 88
Lund, Robert, 70

marine mammals, 80–83
marine parks and oceanariums, 80
Mathews, Dan, 91
McClanahan, Rue, 95
medical research, 19–21, 26, 37–41,
        111–112
    benefits to animals, 40–41
    See also animal research
Merit Award Fur Farm, 99
Moore, Mary Tyler, 92

National Association for Biomedical
        Research (NABR), 19, 115
National Cancer Institute, 30
National Zoo, Washington, D.C., 79
natural law, definition of, 11
natural resources, 51–53, 57, 106
Newkirk, Ingrid, 16, 41, 111
nutria, **114**
nutrition, 43–46
    of nonvegetarian diet, 55–56
    of vegetarian diet, 50–51

Ocean Park, Cousteau Society, Paris, 84
Ornish, Dean, 46
ozone, 52

Pacheco, Alex, 16
pandas, 81, **82**, 83
People for the Ethical Treatment of
    Animals (PETA), 16, 18, 41, 91, 103
People's Republic of China, 81
pharmaceutical manufacturers, 23, 26–27
Phoenix Zoo, 87
pigeons, hunting of, 65, 70
Pinchot, Gifford, 72
Point Defiance Zoo, Tacoma, Washington,
    87
polio, 38
pound laws, 112
Preakness, 76
Princeton, New Jersey, 70
product safety testing, 23, 26, 41, 105, 113
Public Health Service (PHS), 36
Putting People First, 116

rabbits, **21**, 26, 41
rabies, 40, 66, 73
racism compared to speciesism, 8, 25, 34,
    102
rain forests, damage to, 52, 57, 82
Regan, Tom, 15
research
    See animal research
Revlon, 16, 30
rights, definition of, 10
roadside zoos, **78**, 80, 86
rodeos, 75, **76**
Roosevelt, Theodore, 72
Rowan, Andrew N., 36
Royal Society for the Prevention of Cruelty
    to Animals (RSPCA), 8, 13
Ryder, Richard, 8

salmonella contamination, 50
Salt, Henry, 14
San Clemente island, goat population, 73
San Diego Wild Animal Park, 88
San Diego Zoo, 79
saturated fat, definition of, 50
science, use of animals
    See animal research
Scrafford, Joel, 66
sexism compared to speciesism, 8, 34, 102
"Silver Spring Monkeys," 17
Singer, Peter, 14–15, 104

slavery, 24
speciesism, 8, 15, 102
speciesists, 25
Spira, Henry, 15–16
Stanton, Elizabeth Cady, 103
subject of a life philosophy, 15
suffragists, definition of, 104
Sullivan, Louis H., 118

Taub, Edward, 18
terrorism, 108–110
terrorist organizations, 18–19
thalidomide, 29, 39
traps, 63–64, **67**, 70

University of California at Davis, 19
U.S. Department of Agriculture
    Animal and Plant Health Inspection
        Service, 109
U.S. Department of Agriculture (USDA),
    36
    food guide pyramid, **45**
U.S. Fish and Wildlife Service, 73
U.S. Justice Department
    Criminal Division, 109
utilitarianism, definition of, 14

vegetarianism, 44–46
violence, 19, 92
vivisection, 23
    definition of, 13
    See also dissection, of animals
vivisectionists, 27

Washington National Zoo, 81
Weber, Vin, 116
Wilberforce, William, 13
Wild Canid Survival Center, St. Louis, 87
wildlife agencies, 66, 69
wildlife management, 68, 73
wildlife refuge system, 73
World Society for the Protection of
    Animals, 81
Worldwatch Institute, 52

zoos, 75–90
    See also animals as entertainment